**Volume 2 in the "Magic of" Series**

# THE MAGIC
## OF
# PAST LIFE THERAPY

**By**

# RICHARD A. GREENE

**Advanced Hypnotic Resources,
Strategies and Techniques for the Attainment
of Personal Power, Self-Healing and
Valuable Personal Resources.**

PH/NEXT STEP PUBLICATIONS

A 'Magic Of' BOOK - Volume 2

Published by
Next Step Publications, Inc.
P.O. Box 1403
Nashua, New Hampshire 03061

ISBN: 0-942783-03-4

Printed by arrangement with Next Step Publications
Printed in the United States of America
First Printing - 1992

# DEDICATION

This book is dedicated to

# EILEEN RAPPAPORT

- and to all the other members of the Best and the Brightest Club. Here is just a partial list:

Dr. David Alpirn • Connirae and Steve Andreas • Richard Bandler
Gregory Bateson • Gil Boyne • Aleister Crowley • Billy Crystal
Dwight Damon • Robert Dilts • Elsom Eldridge • Milton Erickson
Fate Magazine et al • Ramona Garcia • Uri Geller • Steven Gilligan
John Grinder • L. Ron Hubbard • Mark Hughes • "Magic" Johnson
Ray Krise • Steve and Jill LaVelle • Lewellyn Publishing et al
Shirley McLaine • Virginia K. Miller • Dr. Charles Rappaport
Israel Regardie • Wilhelm Reich • Tony Robbins • Scott D. Rogo
Yephrem Shubanoff • Dr. Bernie Siegal • Dick Sutphen • James E. Tolleson
• Samuel Weiser Inc. et al

# TABLE OF CONTENTS

**PAGE**

INTRODUCTION. . . . . . . . . . . . . . . . . . . . . . . . . . . . . . . . . . . . . . . . . 1

CHAPTER 1  - PAST LIFE THERAPY - ADVANCED THERAPY. . . . . 4

CHAPTER 2  - THE MIND AND HOW IT WORKS . . . . . . . . . . . . . . . 12

CHAPTER 3  - HOW PAST LIFE RECALL & THERAPY WORKS. . . . 25

CHAPTER 4  - PAST LIFE RECALL METHODS. . . . . . . . . . . . . . . . . .37

CHAPTER 5  - INTRODUCTION TO PAST LIFE THERAPY. . . . . . . .54

CHAPTER 6  - PAST LIFE THERAPY METHODS. . . . . . . . . . . . . . . . 67

CHAPTER 7  - CHECKING YOUR WORK. . . . . . . . . . . . . . . . . . . . . 80

CHAPTER 8  - ACCESSING NEW BEHAVIORS, TALENTS
                      AND RESOURCES WITH PLT. . . . . . . . . . . . . . . . . .85

CHAPTER 9  - OVERCOMING PAIN WITH PLT. . . . . . . . . . . . . . . . 93

CHAPTER 10 - PERSONAL POWER WITH PLT. . . . . . . . . . . . . . . . .99

CHAPTER 11 - HEALING WITH PLT. . . . . . . . . . . . . . . . . . . . . . . . . 104

CHAPTER 12 - THE PATTERNS OF PAST LIVES. . . . . . . . . . . . . . . 114

CHAPTER 13 - HANDLING PLT DIFFICULTIES. . . . . . . . . . . . . . . .126

CHAPTER 14 - CHANGING THE FUTURE/RELIVING THE PAST. . . 131

CHAPTER 15 - OTHER POSSIBILITIES OF PLT. . . . . . . . . . . . . . . . 136

APPENDIX 1 - THE TERMINOLOGY OF PLT. . . . . . . . . . . . . . . . . . 146

CATALOG . . . . . . . . . . . . . . . . . . . . . . . . . . . . . . . . . . . . . . . . . . . C-1

# Introduction

Past Life Recall and Past Life Therapy are dynamic therapeutic techniques that can relieve most people of unwanted physical, mental and emotional problems and patterns in record time.

These techniques to recall Past Lives are literally psychological dynamite. Many people using traditional psychology, medical or psychiatric therapy are told that such therapy is not rapid and that it can take many years to overcome present psychological blocks and problems.

Past Life therapy reduces years of therapy down to hours and minutes. The material presented in this book will teach you to use Past Life Therapy for both yourselves and others. Once these simple and easy-to-use methods are committed to memory and you have had a chance to use them, you will find that most problems can be relieved in less than 15 minutes flat. (This, of course, depends on the ability and skills of yourself and those of your client.)

In fact, I have used these techniques in waiting rooms, buses, airplanes and even during meetings. When I found myself confronted by some difficulty or problem that could affect my actions or the outcome of a business negotiation or deal, I would use the PLT® methods described in this book to change and alter my behavior and attitude. With my new behavior and attitude, the negotiations would work out, favorably for both myself and the other party.

In relationships, I found how easy it is to get along with other people by understanding how I have known them from the past. I would simply zip back into 3 or 4 lifetimes where I knew the person, and see the kind of relationships that we had. From that information, I could easily predict the kind of relationship, activities and attitudes we would share in this life.

I also use PLT® to alter areas of difficulties, bad communication, or just about anything else that bothers me or makes my life difficult, by recalling my past life with that person. While reviewing the past life, I review the events that happened then, which are also the events that are causing the present life time problems. By the mere act of recalling and reviewing the past life, the present life problems simply disappear.

Finally, this book is about you. It will show you how to handle all your present problems and change them for the better.

• You will learn to alter your awareness and thereby alter your behavior.

• You will discover why you now know and how you once knew the people who are in your life now.

• You will discover that many people you work with now, you once knew (for good or bad) in the past.

Once the scenario is observed and the past life relationship is discovered and remembered (brought back from the unconscious mind to the conscious awareness), it becomes fun and informative to see how the past life dynamics are still unfolding in present time. For example, you can learn why your boss favors some and disdains others, or why your lover irks you!

Using the Past Life Therapy and Recall techniques, you will also learn to recall incidents and events of this life as well. What was your birth actually like? You can remember quite easily. You will discover for yourself things that you did quite easily in your youth that today may be now consciously forgotten.

There is nothing mystical or "occult" about Past Life Therapy. In fact, there is only your conscious mind and your unconscious mind. Whether you are Christian, Muslim, Atheist or Buddhist, this material works the same for all people if you let it. When you use PLT, you are using the functioning of the body and mind. There is nothing in this material that trespasses one's belief in religion. All religions state that you are a spiritual and eternal soul. Many religions also state that you may have been around more often than just one time, one body. This truth and more data than you can possibly conceive possible at his time, are in this book. Actually this data is within you and by using PLT, you can unlock this information.

Imagine recalling a past life and seeing the life style you once lived. You will discover, amazingly enough, so many parallel situations between your present lifestyle and the one that you lived then. You will notice that many of your present life goals and philosophies stem from past lives. The people you meet in this life and who have an impact on you are ones you have known before.

But don't believe me, try these techniques yourself. This is the only way that you will ever know if Past Life Therapy really works or not. You will see and experience rapid positive changes in as many areas of your life as you apply this knowledge.

May you never be the same!

Richard A. Greene
P.O. Box 1403
Nashua, NH 03061

# Chapter 1

## Past Life Therapy -
## Advanced Therapy of the Mind

### *TALES OF PAST LIFE THERAPY*

#### Harriet and Paralysis

One morning in early March 1981, Harriet of Brookline, Massachusetts awoke to find her left hand totally paralyzed. She immediately checked into a Boston hospital where doctors examined her and made countless lab tests. After she had spent four days in the hospital, the physicians threw up their hands. They had no idea what had happened to Harriet nor did they know whether she would ever use her hand again. All they knew was that her left hand, for some unknown reason, showed serious nerve damage (200 centimeters).

One doctor estimated, that at best, she might regain use of her

4

hand in eight to 10 months. A physical therapist who claimed to have seen cases like this before, told Harriet she would never recover its use.

Harriet was left-handed and these gloomy prognoses were terribly frightening. She decided not to accept them. She came to me for healing using Past Life Therapy.

On her first visit, her hand and arm were icy and blue as they had been when she first checked into the hospital. She could not move her fingers, hand or arm. I helped her to return to past lives to uncover the reason behind her health problem. During our session, she remembered a past lifetime where she was in a relationship with a man that she loved. He was going to walk out on her. She begged him not to. In order to prove her love for him, she picked up a cutting tool and cut her left arm off at the upper arm. As she remembered this, her face relaxed and calmed. She had some sort of inner awareness.

"Oh, this is just like what happened this time!"

"What do you mean?" I asked.

"Well, my boyfriend threatened to leave me (this lifetime) just before this paralysis occurred. Then I woke up with my body bloated and my left arm paralyzed. It happened now just like then. Only this time I did not cut off my arm. My mind did that by paralyzing it.", she said.

She had a release. This is a total erasure of the emotion and negative energy locked in the body and mind. This energy is associated with the past lifetime. (See the past life therapy terminology listed in the appendix in the back of the book.)

I asked her to be back in present time.

Once she did that, I asked her to move her left hand. What had been previously impossible for her to do, she did easily. **She moved her fingers.**

In less than three weeks, Harriet had total control of her hand and arm back.

### Lori and the Benign Tumor

Lori came to my office by referral. She could not bend over as she had a mass growing on her right pelvic bone. Just sitting was painful, never mind walking or moving fast. Bending over to touch her toes was an impossible task. The pain was too excruciating.

Lori told me that her family doctor had conducted ultrasound tests and discovered the growth on her right pelvic bone. He immediately told her that surgery was necessary. She asked if it would go away by itself. The doctor said that would require a miracle. And he stressed that would not happen. He also said that although her pelvic mass was benign now, it could go malignant and so surgery was necessary immediately.

Before agreeing to surgery, she came to me. We discussed her problem. I then had her relax and go back into the past life that was the primary incident for her present pelvic tumor. As she recalled the past life, the issues were around her husband and herself and their marriage. She cognited that there was a tremendous amount of guilt from having betrayed her husband in a past life. Some of the things that she was doing now in the present life, she suddenly realized also made her feel guilty, as if she were betraying him still.

After she cognited on that past life experience and what had

6

happened then and realized how it affected her in her present life, she had her release. She told me that she felt as if something just snapped and she wanted to test it. She stood up and started to bend over as if to touch her toes. She was amazed that there was no pain whatsoever. She bent over and touched her toes several times.

Lori was kind enough to give me her doctor's letter. In the beginning of the letter, he states that there is no significant difference. At the end of the letter, he states that there is no mass. How can this be? Was the growth a misdiagnosis that the doctor was trying to cover up? Is this a doctor trying to cover his misdiagnosis? What about the fact that the patient, Lori, couldn't even move without pain? But after our session, she bent over and touched her toes?

### Linda and Cancer

Linda came to me by referral. She had problems with keeping her balance and she suffered excruciating pain whenever she tried to have sex. Her doctor did a pap smear test on her. When it was returned from the laboratory where it was sent for analysis, the return was a "5." This indicated invasive cancer of her uterus. The doctor summarily announced that she needed a hysterectomy.

Linda was a young woman with no children yet. Certainly, the hysterectomy would have destroyed any and all chances of having children. She went to another doctor for a second opinion. He took a pap smear as well. When the results came back from the laboratory it again indicated a "5" after this second test. This was when Linda came to me.

She came for her appointment accompanied by her husband. He sat patiently as I worked with Linda. In this case, we tried past life work. Nothing seemed to come up and nothing seemed to release from her consciousness. I then had her scan and review times and incidents of this present life. The incident came up that when she was about 16 years, she had sex with a boy about her age who was forceful and aggressive. He touched her in the sexual area, but with such force as to hurt her.

As she remembered that incident, she suddenly showed all the signs of a release. Her face loosened up, she relaxed more. As she lightened up, she felt some strange but comfortable feelings in her lower stomach and sexual area. She looked at me and said, "I think it is gone!"

Linda left my office looking good, feeling great and optomistic about the future.

About 5 days later, Linda called me on the phone. She was glum. "What's happening?" I asked.

Linda replied sadly, "After I saw you, the very next day I went back to my doctor. I had him do another pap test. He sent it out to the laboratory. It came back and it still indicated a "5." I was so sure that we had handled this."

Suddenly, Linda got an insight. "Maybe the tests don't respond to sudden changes right away! I know, I'll call the laboratory" she said.

Linda called me back about an hour later.

"I talked with a technician at the lab. He said that even if cancer were to suddenly go into remission, it would take about four to 5 weeks for the new skin cells to grow in." Linda said excitedly. "So I'll wait 4 weeks and then have another pap test."

Linda waited the four weeks. That's when I got a phone call from her. She said laughingly, "It's a "2." The pap smear taken at that time came back from the laboratory changed. "2" means that it reduced to a bacterial infection.

Linda came back for one final session. About 4 weeks later I received a letter from her that stated, "The results are now a "1." The "1" indicated total healing and normal cell tissues.

## <u>PAST LIFE THERAPY</u>

Past Life Therapy (PLT) is an advanced therapeutic technique. In many cases, the PLT mental technology techniques can fully handle a person's problem many times in just one session! Compare this to traditional therapy, which can take years, and I'm sure you can see the power that this technique generates.

It is important to understand that PLT, like any science or therapy, works well in the hands of a well-trained and skilled PLT therapist. But PLT possesses the same limits that confront most therapies and therapists, the fundamental one being: **"If the client does not want to change, then he will not change!"** This is an affirmation that only the client has the power in this therapy. The client can go as fast or as slow as he desires. This is because the client does this therapy to himself.

Therefore, **the first prerequisite of PLT is that the client must be willing to handle and resolve the problem.** This is true even if you use PLT for yourself only.

In hypnosis, there is a statement that "All Hypnosis Is Self-Hypnosis." What this means is that the person has the power to change, not the hypnotist. And since all power is within the client, the hypnotist's main role is as a guide and teacher. With PLT, the past life therapist acts as a guide and teacher. The client actually heals himself via the techniques.

PLT is much like hypnosis in both content and context. The very act of looking to your internal mental memories and visual pictures and listening to your internal voices constitutes a hypnotic trance state.

Some people argue that there is a difference between past life recall and hypnosis. There are others who state that past life therapy is simply hypnosis and nothing else. My experience is that past life therapy and hypnosis are both hypnotic and result in trance induction. In hypnosis, a trance is deliberately induced. In past life therapy, a trance is induced by the very act of recalling the past life.

Regardless of the thoughts and ideas that you may have about past life therapy, I have found it best to adopt the following attitude:

*"Whether or not past lives exist is not important. Whether or not the past lives evoked by past life therapy is real or imagined is unimportant. What does matter is that PLT works. As long as PLT works and works faster, more elegantly and efficiently than any other therapy that you have ever tried, as long as it clears up your problems, your student's problems and your client's problems faster than anything they have ever tried before and does it safely, and permanently, then it does not matter if past lives are real or imagined! (You will learn why later!)"*

### WHAT PLT IS NOT

PLT is mental dynamite. It is not a toy. It is not a process to allow a client with a lousy present life to escape into fantasy by indulging in being another personality. In fact, it is unimportant whether one was a janitor or a Napoleon. It is only important to handle the client's present time problem by allowing the client access to his own internal resources so that he can solve his problem.

Now that you have had an introduction to Past Life Therapy, let's move on to Chapter 2 - "The Mind and How It Works."

# Chapter 2

## The Mind and How It Works

Essentially, there are two parts to the mind. The conscious mind and the subconscious (or unconscious) mind. This chapter will show you how these two parts work for the betterment or detriment of your life.

### THE CONSCIOUS MIND

The conscious mind is the analytical, rational, logical mind. In our present technological society, it is the part of our awareness that we tend to use the most. Technology and science establishes itself on the laws of logic. This logic is attributed to the conscious mind.

Now, the conscious mind is considered by psychologists to be only one-tenth of the potential possible for man. It has also been theorized that if man were capable of using more of his consciousness, he would possess incredible and unusual powers, supernatural in scope.

12

## CONSCIOUS MIND FUNCTIONING

The one-tenth conscious mind thinks in words. When you close your eyes, and pay attention to your mind, you can hear thoughts in the form of words flow through your conscious mind.

## NOTICE THAT YOU DO NOT SEE THESE WORDS! YOU ONLY HEAR THEM!

These words may fly through your consciousness as sentences, phrases or even single words. This is known as the internal dialogue and is auditory in nature. To prove this to yourself, try the following exercise:

Think about some chore that you have to perform today, such as grocery shopping. As you think analytically about it, how does it come to your mind? Pictures may appear, but you will notice that there are also thoughts which manifest in the form of words and internal conversation or dialogue.

The conscious mind is linear and logical. One formula that can best express the functioning of the conscious mind is: if a=b and b=c then a=c. Perfectly, straight logical thinking.

If we think in the way that the conscious mind thinks, then we are using the conscious mind. For instance, since the conscious mind thinks in words, should you think in words exclusively, then you are using the conscious mind.

## Experiment #1

In order to better understand the conscious mind and how it works, try this exercise. Think the following words:

"I want my hand to touch my shoulder."

Think this word phrase over and over again. As you do this, you are using the conscious mind. After about 15 repetitions of this phrase, look at your right hand and notice if a change has occurred.

You will probably notice that nothing has happened. Your hand did not move in the slightest. No matter how much you may have had an urge to move your hand it did not rise up and touch your shoulder.

This is an example of the power of the conscious, analytical, one-tenth mind that is glorified by science and technology. It could not even move your hand.

In other words, if we followed admonitions to live our lives in total logic, then we would not even be capable of moving our bodies. We would be vegetables. After all, you couldn't move your hand could you?

## HOW THE SUBCONSCIOUS MIND WORKS

We do however, move our bodies. Since it is not the worded, thought processes of the analytical mind that cause the body to move, then we must be using another method and another part of the mind in order to make the body move. If the answer does not lie in the one-tenth conscious mind, then it must lie in the remaining nine-tenths subconscious mind. Let us explore that part of the mind now.

Begin by moving your right arm up and down. Now, just close your eyes and concentrate your attention on your mind. Try to perceive what is happening in your mind as your arm moves up and down. (You may not be able to perceive what is happening right away.) Try this exercise for about three minutes.

What you may (or may not) have noticed is that as you moved your right arm up and down, you had images or pictures in your mind (of your hand rising up and down) even as your hand moved up and down. These mental pictures are a function of the subconscious mind.

To better understand the subconscious mind, try the following exercises:

1) Imagine a glass of water. How does it come to your mind? In other words, in what manner or form is it presented to your mind?

2) Recall a time when you drank a glass of water. How does it come to your consciousness? In other words, in what manner does it appear to your consciousness?

3) Recall a dream that you once had. How does it come to your consciousness. In other words, in what manner does it appear to your consciousness?

In all the cases given above, you noticed that the form in which all things came to your mind was in the form of pictures and images. Again, this helps to show you that the subconscious mind thinks in pictures. Further, imagination, memory, dreams, and ESP or psychic experiences all occur in pictures or images. Because of this, these functions are all considered to be part of the subconscious mind.

Another important fact or observation about the subconscious mind is that it never sleeps. While you are sleeping, the conscious mind becomes dormant; that is, it turns off. The subconscious mind however, does not turn off. This is best shown by the fact that dreams, which are a part of the functioning subconscious mind, occur while in the sleep state. After all, dreams are visual and that part of the mind which is visual is the subconscious mind.

The subconscious is always active and working whether the conscious mind is awake or not. While you are asleep, your heart keeps beating and you keep breathing. Obviously, it is not the sleeping conscious mind that is controlling those functions.

Another point which indicates that the subconscious mind is indeed working while the conscious mind is unconscious has been demonstrated on the operating table. Many doctors now realize that when a patient is on the operating table and anaesthesized, it does not mean he is totally unconscious. It only means that the conscious mind is unconscious. That is, the conscious mind is not analyzing and rationalizing as it would normally.

Walk up to someone who is unconscious and ask him or her how much 2+2 is. They will not answer. This lack of communication while unconscious, caused many doctors to believe that the patient was out cold completely and could not be conscious in the least. However, this only indicates that a portion of the individuals consciousness, the analytical, logical, conscious mind is not working.

The subconscious mind, however, is always busy and aware. Since the subconscious mind thinks in pictures, it is actually, very much like a camera, always taking pictures. This means that the subconscious mind of the patient on the operating table is taking pictures of the entire operation, hearing everything that is being said as well. Now, because the conscious mind is knocked out, chances are that the person will not remember what was said or done during the operation. However, the events that did occur are indelibly recorded in the individual's memory records (or time film as I call it). With the proper techniques, such as past life therapy, these memories can be recalled to conscious mind clarity.

The subconscious mind is a camera. It records, in pictures, all that is happening around a person. The analytical conscious mind screens and analyzes what is being recorded in the subconscious picture. For instance, when you walk into a room, the subconscious mind takes pictures of the room while the conscious mind analyzes what is present there in the room. As you look at a wall, the subconscious mind takes a picture of the wall and the conscious mind recognizes and analyzes that the wall is indeed a wall. You may or may not be aware of all of the analysis that the conscious mind does, for it all happened quickly. You may or may not be aware of all the "picture taking" that the subconscious mind does, as it happens so quickly.

## HOW THE CONSCIOUS AND UNCONSCIOUS MINDS WORK TOGETHER

Right now, feel the temperature of the room. Is the room hot or cold? Is it just right? If so, how do you know that the room is warm, cold or just right? You are comparing your present environment right now, with other environments that you have experienced in the past. For instance, you know it is warm in the present environment because you have experienced cold in other environments. This act of comparison is always occurring. Unless of course the conscious mind is put out of activity!

You can see then that there are two different types of minds:

1. the conscious, analytical mind that thinks logically in words and sentences.

2. the subconscious mind that thinks primarily in pictures or images.

## HOW THE CONSCIOUS MIND AFFECTS THE UNCONSCIOUS MIND

The conscious and unconscious minds work together. This next example will show you how. Quickly say to yourself the following words:

o house

o cat

o tree

o book

o car

What did you notice happening in your internal consciousness? Pictures! The conscious mind works with words. But each word as it is perceived by the conscious mind is then translated by the subconscious mind into a corresponding picture(s) or an image(s).

This, by the way, is the basic problem regarding all communication. While one person talks of a hardcover book, the other person in the conversation might have a mental picture of a paperback book. Yet another person may have a corresponding picture of an encyclopedia. The same word "Book" gives rise to differing mental images.

This is the process by which all miscommunications are formed. Without a specific definition of what a word means, all people involved in the communication will add their own insight, responses, and mental images/pictures.

Now the conscious mind is actually a filter. It filters the information that has been communicated. For example, the conscious mind becomes aware of words that are spoken. Then the subconscious mind generates a mental picture to correspond with the word. Interestingly enough, the mental picture generated is either one that was experienced or remembered. For instance, in response to the word "book," you may notice a mental image of a book that you own, or it may be one that you saw once.

## HOW THE CONSCIOUS AND UNCONSCIOUS MINDS WORK AGAINST EACH OTHER

In many cases, the two minds are at odds. And here is one helpful hint: **WHENEVER THE TWO MINDS ARE IN CONFLICT, THE SUBCONSCIOUS MIND WINS!**

One example of this conflict is when a person consciously wants to be successful and wealthy. Yet he sabotages his possibilities each and every time. Here the conscious mind is filled with one desire (to be successful and wealthy), but the unconscious mind trips it up. Perhaps the unconscious mind knows that if the person was to be wealthy and successful, he might do something that could end up hurting himself. And so in this case, the subconscious mind is actually helping the person to survive by sabotaging his conscious mind goals.

Does this conflict mean that the person can never be wealthy or successful? Of course not. It simply means that the subconscious mind must be dealt with in order to:

o find out why it is causing this conflict

o uncover what problems from this conflict need to be resolved

o discern if there is some way in which wealth and success can be obtained that is suitable and acceptable to the unconscious mind.

PLT provides the possibilities to do just that!

## THE TIME FILM

I would like to introduce you now to your "Time Film." All memory and sensory representations are actually attached to pictures/ images in the mind. Theses pictures and images make up a "film", called the Time Film.

Like any other film, the Time Film can be fast forwarded, reversed, stopped, played in slow motion, played without sound, played with sound and much more. In fact, in order to remember something that happened to you last week, you basically rewind the Time Film to when the incident happened last week, and then run it forwards. Of course, the mind can do this so fast, there seems to be no forward or reverse going on. But you will see how all this works by the time you finish this book.

Recall eating breakfast this morning. What was the duration (how much time did it take?) of the event?

Now recall the event again. Notice what happens.

Recall the event a third time.

Again notice what happens.

Each time you recalled the event, you may have noticed these results:

o it became easier to recall the event

o you could recall it faster

o most importantly, you remembered more details.

Notice also that as you reviewed the event it was like watching a movie. Once the actions were presented in picture form, you saw only the events and details that took place. You did not see things that did not happen. Nowhere in your recall of the event did an elephant walk through your kitchen. You saw only the details. Just like a movie, no matter how many times you watch it, the actors do not suddenly change lines or act out of character.

You can now see that your memory itself is much like a movie. If you need further proof try these exercises:

Recall a time when you:

o drove a car

o watched TV

o were angry

o had a good time

o went shopping

Notice that all your memories came to you in the form of pictures and images. Pictures and images are the primary representation of memory. Auditory memories are also possible although they are usually associated to your visual memories. For example, if someone suddenly screamed while you were eating lunch, chances are you will recall the scream as you recall eating lunch.

The third way in which memory is associated to pictures is that of physical feeling. Let's say you felt sick at Thanksgiving dinner.

When you remember the Thanksgiving dinner, you will see the pictures, but you will also remember the physical feeling of being stuffed.

So then all memory works in primarily three ways:

1) pictures/images

2) sound/auditory

3) feeling/emotions/kinesthetics

There are also two secondary representations. I call them "secondary" because they are used so infrequently when it comes to memory. These secondary representations are:

4) smell/olfactory  (i.e., the scent of perfume of your dearest love).

5) taste/gustatory (i.e., the taste of champagne).

As you may have noticed, all memory is represented by one or more of the five physical senses. Every piece of memory that you have is first recorded in pictures/images and other sensory representations are associated to the pictures.

Some people claim not to have visual representations. These are the people who claim not to dream or be able to visualize. Actually, the images and pictures are there, but for whatever reason, those pictures lie outside of the person's conscious awareness. Rather than working through visual images, these people use other sensory representations such as feelings or internal voices and dialogues.

For instance, a person who does not see pictures in his mind, may get "feelings" in the pit of his stomach. In this case, the representation of feelings and kinesthetics is the primary way that the person recalls his memory. By addressing the client's feelings/kinesthetics first, usually the pictures will suddenly appear, much to the surprise of the client.

Now that you understand how the two parts of the mind - the conscious and the subconscious minds work together, and how the time film works, let's move on to Chapter 3 and How Past Life Recall and Therapy Work!

# C h a p t e r 3

## How Past Life Therapy Works

Past life therapy works by gaining access to deep memory pictures and scenarios contained within the mind. Right now as you read this book, you have memories of distant times and places. In these memories as well, there are images and pictures of you -- perhaps as an Arab or a Greek, male or female (sometimes possibly an animal), even memories of living on other planets and having different bodies than those presently seen on planet Earth.

Understand that these scenarios, which we refer to as past lives, are influencing and affecting you right now even though you may not have the slightest inkling as to what past lives scenarios exist in your awareness. It doesn't matter whether or not you believe in past lives.

How you do something, whether you do it well or whether you do it poorly, depends on the pictures and past life scenarios in your awareness. As you learned in Chapter 2, there are two minds -- the conscious mind and the unconscious (also called the subconscious) mind. What is in the unconscious mind actually controls the way in which a person sees and perceives life. Therefore, the way to stop the control that a past life scenario in the unconscious mind has on a person now, is to make the unconscious mind scenario conscious. In other words, one must delve into their own unconscious mind looking at it with conscious awareness. This has the effect of releasing the past life scenario and its control on the perceptions of the person.

A past life memory is similar to your regular memory of this life. In some cases, the past life memory may seem deeper or three dimensional. Within each past life scenario, there are events that are both pleasant and unpleasant. The pleasant scenarios and events are not what messes you up or creates your unwanted behaviors. These experiences generate good and pleasant feelings. On the reverse, the negative experiences cause pain and inability to handle life.

To bring a past life into conscious awareness, you only need to view it with full conscious attention. This brings the lifetime from hidden unconsciousness to clear, conscious awareness. By bringing the past lifetime into conscious awareness, the impact and effects of the past life are released from the unconscious mind. After releasing a past life scenario, (by viewing it with conscious attention and awareness), the person attains total freedom from unwanted patterns and habits that were originally caused in that life time. (This is covered in greater detail in Chapter 5.)

To better understand how the unconscious past life patterns and scenarios control our attitudes, perceptions, and beliefs, let's learn how the unconscious mind controls the autonomic systems of the body.

First, let's ask these questions. How do you know when to breathe? And how do you know how to breathe? When you go to sleep at night, what causes your body to breathe while your conscious mind is asleep?

Another question. When you cut your hand, what causes your hand to heal?

A third question. When you are frightened, what causes you to be frightened?

The answer to all the questions above is your unconscious mind. This mind, which is unknown to the conscious mind, runs your body. Before you consciously become aware of fear, the unconscious mind has already increased the flow of adrenalin, changed the breathing, caused a flushing in the face, and prepares the body for fight or flight. After the unconscious mind does all of this, then the conscious mind realizes that it is afraid. But only after the fact. So in other words, the unconscious mind acts before the conscious mind even recognizes what is happening. This is true for all things. For example, is there anything that you do really bad? I mean, is there anything that you simply cannot do or that you wish you could do well, but don't? If so, you will discover that the unconscious mind has a scenario within it that you cannot do that particular task well at all!

In other words, it takes as much planning and organizing and energy and resources to do something bad as it does to do something well. Anything that you do bad or poorly requires you to have mental pictures showing that you cannot do the things as well as you want to.

On the other hand, is there anything that you do really well? In this case, there is a scenario in the unconscious mind that you are skillfully using your energy and resources. Whether or not you fully understand how the unconscious mind works, the important point is that if there is anything that you wish to do excellently, skillfully and powerfully, you must have the proper scenario in the unconscious mind. All activities that you do, you do only as well as your internal unconscious pictures and scenarios allow you to do.

### *Example #1*

Let's take an example of you walking. You know how to walk. But try the following:

**o Walk back and forth across your room several times.** As you walk back and forth, notice what is going on in your mind. Now sit down.

While you were walking, were you thinking about the tightening and untightening of your muscles? The thoughts and pictures in your mind of you walking? The various feelings in your physical body as you walked step by step? The beating of your heart? Your breathing? And all the myriad other things that were going on as you walked back and forth?

It's unlikely! The conscious mind is incapable of keeping track of so many factors in something as simple as walking. Yet these changes did go on in your body. And they were all controlled by your unconscious mind. The unconscious mind can handle (and does handle) perhaps billions of computations and changes in the body no matter how large or miniscule.

The very act of walking however is relegated to the unconscious mind. That act of walking is therefore an unconscious activity. Even the simplest act of moving your arm is actually an unconscious act. You do not really know how you do it, you just do. You can walk, because you learned to do it unconsciously; that is, at the unconscious mind level.

This is especially true for when you first learned to ride a bike, or ice skate or ski. You can do them now because they are unconscious mind acts. You do not know how you do them, but you do.

Now that you understand that what you do well is programmed into the unconscious mind, you should be able to also realize that what you do poorly is also programmed into the unconscious mind.

When you are afraid to speak in front of hundreds of people, your unconscious mind knows exactly what to do to make you afraid. Your conscious mind has very little to do with your actual fear.

But how did your unconscious mind become programmed to do things well or to do them poorly?

**Past lives are the answer.**

## _HOW PAST LIFE THERAPY WORKS_

The way in which past life recall and therapy works is quite simple. Within your unconscious mind are a set of scenarios (past lives). Whether or not you believe in past lives does not matter. Whether or not the past lives actually happened doesn't matter either. If these scenarios are in your unconscious mind, then you act on them, whether consciously or unconsciously.

By simply recalling the specific incident in the past lifetime that is the cause for the present time problem, the impact of the incident releases so that you never act or react in the unwanted way or manner that you have in your present life.

About 99.9% of all present time problems come from an earlier time. That is, they have their beginning in an earlier lifetime. By recalling the lifetime consciously, you actually release the incident. This is why recalling the past life incident erases the present time problem or difficulty.

One argument that can be used for the validity of past life therapy is that I have worked with clients who have been in therapy with a therapist, psychiatrist or psychologist for years trying to solve a particular problem. The therapist or psychiatrist would work with the client's early present lifetime. (Even therapists understand the therapeutic aspect of having a patient return to the original incident. The problem with conventional therapists is that they think that all present time difficulties and behaviors come from this lifetime only.)

When the clients first came to me, they wanted help for some problem that didn't go away or get handled with conventional therapy. When I suggested past life work, they balked at it, and said, "Oh, I already know where the problem comes from!"

Well guess what! If they actually knew where the problem came from, then they wouldn't have the problem anymore. If psychiatrists and therapists guided their clients to the actual incident or event that causes the present time problem, the present time problem would disappear.

A basic law of past life therapy is that the way a person acts, behaves, and handles life in the present time, is based on his past experiences, incidents and understandings. In some cases, (very few though), the incidents and experiences stem from this lifetime. Those clients whose problems have originated in this lifetime, are the ones whose problems clear up fast by reviewing only present lifetime incidents and occurences.

## *HOW THE PAST INFLUENCES THE PRESENT*

This tale is based on a true experience. It will show you the workings of the mind and the process of how an original negative incident leads to illnesses or disorders - regardless of whether the illness is organic or psychosomatic.

A girl, about 8 years old, is riding her bike and she pulls out into the street. Along comes a speeding car. The driver sees the child but cannot stop the vehicle in time. He jams the brake pedal which causes the car to skid and hit the bicycle. The girl is thrown from the bicycle due to the impact of the car. She has the sensation of the environment blurring past her as she is thrown through the air three feet, and then her head hits the pavement with such force as to cause unconsciousness.

Now the girl is a woman at the age of 38, thirty years after the incident. As a grown woman she suffers from almost constant severe headaches. She goes to a doctor who prescribes medicine but that does not eliminate her headaches. The doctor advises the woman to have her head X-rayed in order to see if there is a tumor or any other abnormal growth that could be causing the headaches. Nothing is discovered.

Referring back to the incident, when the girl was 8 years old, her conscious mind went unconscious. Her subconscious mind took over, acting as a movie camera recording sights and sounds such as: the crowd, the car, the ambulance, and the statements made by others (and much more) in the form of pictures and internal audio dialogue. It also recorded the intense pain and shock and the regions of the body that suffered the shock and pain.

All it now takes to awaken that pain (in the form of migraine headaches) in the woman is to hear a loud siren. Other triggers might be a crowd of people, moving fast enough through the environment so that everything she sees is a blur. In other words, any item that was found in the original incident, will awaken the incident and the pain at the unconscious and then conscious mind levels. All she needs to do is perceive the trigger. (More on triggers later.)

The whole period of unconsciousness is recorded as a very precise and clear record of all that happened by the unconscious mind. The only problem is that the conscious mind, once recovered, does not know that this data even exists. It is this hidden data, that is out of the reach of the conscious mind, that causes the illnesses, and discomfort.

Now when a trigger (something which is in the present environment that was also present in the earlier environment when the original accident occurred) sets in, the subconscious mind, without awareness, control or interference from the conscious mind, connects the triggers from the present environment to the past incident. The subconscious mind will then run the incident just as if it was a movie deep in the unconscious mind. Everything in the incident will be played back, but most especially the pain will be turned on. For instance, after the girl was knocked down, she may have had a hard time breathing. Suddenly, she finds herself having a hard time breathing. The illness or discomforts (headaches, difficult breathing) occurs because the subconscious mind brings all the elements of the original event into play.

Sometimes just reaching a certain age can bring on illness and pain. Other times a particular fear or aversion may come to the surface. For instance, a person who may never have had a fear of water earlier in life, suddenly at the age of 35 becomes fearful of large bodies of water. Largely this is due to a past life incident where the person had a painful incident or loss involving water, such as drowning, in a past life at the age of 35.

## THE THREE MAJOR AREAS OF LIFE

There are essentially three areas of human existence that contains the problem incident which in turn contains the trigger that is the cause for illness. They are:

1) Early childhood
2) Prenatal-in the mother's womb-incidents
3) Past life incidents.

Many people, when asked to recollect things that they did prior to the age of 5 years old, can not remember significant incidents. This first led psychologists to the belief that memory began at the age of 5 years old; the theory being that the brain and other physical organs at 5 years old was not sufficiently developed enough to record and maintain incidents and events that occurred.

Only until recently, through the use of hypnosis and regression techniques, has it been suggested that an individual can remember before 5 years old. But, in addition, it has also been that the individual can, with the proper techniques, actually recall the birth incident in full; even prenatal events as well.

After a short amount of practice with past life therapy, the individual can recall with startling clarity, every event, both major and small, that made up the birth experience. But that is not all! The individual can recall his or her own prenatal events and experiences with astounding accuracy. Prior to prenatal events comes past lives.

The past life therapist approaches the individual from the viewpoint that he or she is more than just a physical body. He or she is a soul or consciousness, that will depart from the body and continue to exist even after the body dies. This consciousness (the "Real You"):

    o is immortal

    o is not limited by the laws of science

    o retains a memory of over trillions of years. This memory is a complete record of all the events that the immortal being experienced in its travels through existence.

The Past Life Therapist realizes that the mind and the brain are not the same. The brain is similar to the computer hardware and the mind is the software program which tells the brain what to do. The very act of reasoning out problems and difficulties lies in both the hardware (brain) and the software (mind). The way in which a person solves a problem or handles his life is dependent on the way in which the software/mind is set up to deal with it.

## HOW THE MIND GETS PROGRAMMED

How does the mind get programmed?

Basically, in two ways.

1) Directly from experience. For instance, a child bitten by a dog will be naturally afraid of all dogs no matter how friendly or restrained the dogs are.

2) Indirectly through thought transference with others. For example, many people are afraid of snakes. Yet they have never been actually in the presence of one. So why then does a person react or be repulsed by a snake or even the thought of a snake especially when they never had a first hand experience with such a snake?

One answer is that it might be a racial memory. That is, fear of snakes are natural to all people because snakes represent the past from which man evolved.

Upon further inspection using PLT, we discover that fear of snakes occur in individuals due to experiences they had with snakes in past lives. This past life theory explains and brings together many of the loose ended facets, theories, and hypotheses found in psychology and psychiatry.

*If you work with a client and you review present life incidents and that does not release the client from an unwanted behavior or pattern, then the original incident that is the source for the problem must stem from an earlier incident. That earlier incident will be discovered to be in a past lifetime.*

One of the reasons why conventional psychologists and psychiatrists do not get the high number of cures that they should is because they are only looking at the client's early present life childhood memory. To a time perhaps when daddy spanked or scolded the client. They don't get the client to go back far enough to see the original incident. Therefore, the problem doesn't resolve.

What is needed is to get the client to move to the earlier lifetime and the original incident. How to do this is covered in the next chapter, so let's move on to Chapter 4 - Past Life Recall Methods.

# Chapter 4

## Past Life Recall Methods

The past life recall techniques that you are about to learn are neither dangerous nor difficult. In fact, remembering past lives is no different than remembering what you did yesterday or several years ago. The most difficulty you may have with recalling past lives is believing that what you are seeing is actually a past life!

There is much misinformation spread about by the ignorant and the fearful about past lives. The most recent piece of misinformation that I heard is that you might get stuck in some past life and not be able to return to present time. This is totally absurd. Past life recall is nothing more than the utilization of your memory. When was the last time that you remembered drinking a cup of coffee on a past saturday morning and got stuck there never to return to the present? You'd be amazed at the stupid concepts and ideas that people have about past life recall and therapy.

## PAST LIFE RECALL AND ASTRAL PROJECTION

These techniques to remember past lives uses the ability known as astral projection. Briefly, astral projection is a simple visualization method by which a person can place his or her consciousness to other locations from outside of the body. This means that instead of looking at your environment through your physical eyes and from the perspective or viewpoint of the physical body, you can witness reality through a higher sense of perception not limited by physical limitations.

Our physical eyes are limited to seeing only within a particular spectrum of color called the visible light spectrum. We cannot perceive the presence of energies and forces that exist outside of the visible spectrum with the unaided eye.

The human ear can only hear within the range of audio sounds approximately 20 to 20,000 cycles per second. Anything above or below this vibratory range cannot be detected by the physical sensory apparatus. Astral projection releases the consciousness itself which can then perceive energies and vibrations outside of these energies which can be detected by the five physical senses. It is because of the higher sensory perceptions available through astral projection that we can perceive past lives. Therefore, it is essential that you learn to use astral projection. It is actually quite simple and safe. (Refer to my book, *The Handbook of Astral Power* published by Next Step Center.)

### ASTRAL PROJECTION TECHNIQUE #1

Try the following technique:

1) Sit relaxed for about 30 seconds. Let your eyes close and simply let your mind relax. Release any and all preconceptions, fears,

or worries.

2) Imagine that inside your physical body is another body that looks the same as your physical body. (This is called the astral body, also known as the duplicate, the double, the KA, and so on, in ancient spiritual literature). This inner astral body may appear to be white in your mind's eye.

3) Imagine that the astral body now leaves your physical body and moves across to the other side of the room.

4) Now in your mind's eye, imagine what it would look like to be on the other side of the room and face your physical body. What does the perspective from this new viewpoint look like to you now?

5) Now imagine that you leave through the door and walk out front of where you live. (You should notice that there are no physical obstacles to the astral body and that you can quite easily move through walls and doors. This is because the astral body, which vibrates faster than physical matter, can interpenetrate and pass through physical matter. Unlike the physical body which vibrates at the same speed as all other matter and is therefore limited by matter.)

6) Now that you have projected to out in front of your house or apartment where you live, look at your building. What or how does it look to you now? (At first you might suspect that it is your memory that you are using and that you are recalling what the building looks like rather than experiencing it at first hand. This is all right for now since this tendency to rely on memory rather than projected sensory perception will eventually fade with practice.)

7) Now look around you. Look to your left and try to perceive whatever you can.

8) Look to your right and preceive whatever you can.

9) Now look behind you and perceive whatever that you can.

10) Now look in front of you again and perceive whatever you can.

Once you have accomplished this, return back to the room where your physical body is located. Then after re-entering the room, return to your physical body. Now merge your astral body and physical body together. Then merge your consciousness and return to normal awareness.

## COMMENTS

The purpose of this first astral excursion is to familiarize you with the manner in which astral projection takes place. In essence, it is only a controlled and concentrated visualization.

You may have noticed that you could depart from your physical body and go out to in front of the house almost immediately. You did not have to take the long way through the door or window and down the steps and so on as your physical body would. By the way, there is no preferenceas to which way is better.

In trying to look behind you, you may have turned the astral body in the same way as you would your physical body. With a little practice however, it becomes quite evident that since the astral body is not physical and it does not rely on the physical eyes for perception, it is possible to perceive information from behind you directly - without need for your body to turn around.

## ASTRAL PROJECTION TECHNIQUE #2

This next technique takes what you have learned and experienced from technique #1 and enhances it to a further ability.

1) Perform all the steps in exercise #1. Now when you are out in front of the house or apartment and after looking all around you, do the following:

a) Envision that you are rising straight up into the air. Continue rising. In your mind's eye, try to get an image of what the buildings look like below you. Try also to see what the neighborhood looks like as if from an airplane or helicopter in the sky.

b) Keep on rising. Ascend further and further up until you leave the planet Earth and keep rising into space. Continue to rise upwards into space for about 5 minutes. When you end your rising, you should try to envision, (if it is not coming to your consciousness immediately) that you are out in space where there are no suns or planets. Just unpopulated space. Allow yourself to stay at this point from about 5 minutes. In other words, let yourself simply "be" at that point in space. Do not let any other worries or thoughts of a mundane or earthly nature invade your mind.

c) After about 5 minutes, start to return to the Earth by simply descending back through space the way in which you came. Allow yourself to come back to the neighborhood where you live until you land in front of the building where you live. Finally, enter into the building and return to the room where your physical body is located. Move the astral body back into the physical body. Then simply return to normal consciousness.

This Ends Technique #2

### COMMENTS

The purpose of this exercise is twofold:

1) to enable you to move to distant planes of awareness of consciousness.

2) the ability to gain a relaxed and clear awareness.

You should notice that the more you go out into space a new feeling appears to come over you. This new feeling may seem to be one of detachment. That is, that your difficulties and obstacles in life reduce to petty problems and become very distant. You will also notice an expanded awareness. If you do not, continue to work with this exercise until you get a feeling of clearheadedness. Once this state of awareness is attained, then you will find success with past life recall/therapy easy to come by.

### PRESENT LIFE MEMORY TECHNIQUE #3

1. Recall something that you ate today.
2. Recall the complete incident of eating.
3. Recall the complete incident again.
4. Finally, once again, recall the incident.

You have now recalled the incident for a total of three times. Did you notice any difference between the first time that you recalled the eating incident and the third time? If so, what type of difference?

You should have noticed that by the third recollection of the memory events, you got more and more detail on what you recalled. Nothing in the event should have changed. For instance, if you were eating donuts, the recollection should not change to eating steak. The movie (in this case, the eating incident recorded in the subconscious mind) should not change one bit. The only 'change' is that there should be more and more detail as you view the incident.

## *PRESENT LIFE REVIEW*

The present life review is meant to enable you to recall the past present life from pre-natal to birth to present time. This should be able to release any present time problems if these do indeed do have their cause in this present life time.

1) Imagine yourself rising up into the air about 500 feet above the ground.

2) Is it light or dark out? If it is dark, turn it to light. If light, turn it to dark.

3) Now if it is light, turn it dark. If dark, turn it to light.

4) Now if it is dark, turn it light. If light, turn it to dark.

5) Now simply decide that you are going to descend from your position above the ground and that when you land you will be back at your 3rd birthday.

6) Descend towards the earth and when you land, you should be back at about or on the day of your third birthday. (Although you may not recognize it as such at first).

7) Notice what time of day it is.

8) Where are you?

9) Are there others around you?

10) What type of clothes are you wearing?

11) What type of clothes are others around you wearing?

12) Now from where you are located in the time memory, proceed to move forward. In other words, if you are at your 3rd

birthday and it is 2:00 in the afternoon, then you need to move forward to 3:00 pm then to 5:00 pm, etc. until you reach the end of the day. So now proceed through the day as best as you can from the time in which you landed. Run through the memory until you reach the time that day ended for you, whenever it was that you fell asleep.

13) After trying to remember as much as you can from the time when you landed, next move back to when the day began for you. This would most likely be when you first woke up. So then move to when you first woke up.

A) What time was it?

B) What did the place you were in look like?

C) Now move through what happened from when you first woke up. Continue on through the memory until you can recall what happened from where you first woke up on your third birthday to when you ended the day or went to sleep.

You might notice that at first the memory comes with difficulty to your consciousness. However, after constant and persistent reviewing, you will notice that the images 'loosen' and become clear. With constant recollection of running from the beginning to the end of the day, you will be able to recall in total the events of the day on your 3rd birthday.

After recollecting your third birthday, move back up into the air about 500 feet above the ground. Now once again, begin to descend but this time land at your 2nd birthday. Do the same as you did for reviewing and recalling you 3rd birthday.

After recalling and reviewing your 2nd birthday, rise up once again about 500 feet into the air and above the ground. Then start to descend. But this time, land in your 1st birthday; then review it as you did your second and third birthdays.

For most people, the instructions given above are enough to cause them to be able to recall and review their early present lifetime birthdays. If you are having any difficulty with these processes, just keep trying. And if you need to, have somebody else ask you the questions. This will enable you to devote full and complete attention on your recall ability.

This recall work that you have done already should be able to prepare you to move back into past lives. I have however added in 3 examples of clients with whom I used this material. This should help offset any questions or problems that you may have.

## RUNNING THE PAST LIFE

Here are some things you should be aware of when you recall or run past lives or specific incidents in past lives. First of all, the life time and all the incidents in that lifetime are like a movie. The past life movie runs from beginning to end. In some cases, the movie can be out of synch so that you jump over specific times and incidents. When this happens to you there is something "missing" in your review of the incident and the lifetime does not release thereby relieving you of the present time problem.

Simply reviewing the incident or lifetime over and over again adds more detail, makes the "movie" clearer and eventually releases the incident/lifetime.

Okay, let's get to work!

## RUNNING THE PAST LIFE

1) Imagine yourself rising up into the air about 500 feet above the ground.

2) Is it light or dark out? If it is dark, turn it to light. If light, turn it to dark.

3) Now if it is light, turn it to dark. If dark, turn it to light.

4) Now if it is dark, turn it to light. If light, turn it to dark.

5) Now simply decide that you are going to descend from your position above the ground and that when you land you will be back in a past life.

6) Descend towards the earth and when you land, you should be back in a past lifetime. (Although you may not recognize it as such at first).

7) Notice what time of day it is.

8) Where are you?

9) Are there others around you?

10) What type of clothes are you wearing?

11) What type of clothes are others around you wearing?

12) Now from where you are located in the time memory, proceed to move forward. In other words, if you are out in the open and it is daytime, move to nighttime. So now proceed through the day as best as you can from the time in which you landed.

13) Move into the future. You can do this by deciding to view the future. You can go a day at a time, a week at a time, a month at a time or even a year or years at a time.

14) Move on to the death of your body in that lifetime. Notice how old your body was when you died. Notice also how you died and

what the causes were for the death of your body. Review this several times.

15) Now, return back to the birth of the body in that lifetime. Notice how you were born, where you were born and who was present at your birth. Review this several times.

16) Finally, run the entire lifetime from birth to death, several times. Pay particular attention to any significant events or incidents that may have occurred. Review the entire lifetime several times.

You might notice that at first the memory comes with difficulty to your consciousness. However, after constant and persistent reviewing, you will notice that the images "loosen-up" and become clear. With constant recollection of running from the birth to death of the lifetime, you will be able to recall in total the events of the past lifetime.

## RUNNING ANOTHER PAST LIFE

After recollecting the past life, move back up into the air about 500 feet above the ground. Now once again, begin to descend but this time decide to land in an even earlier lifetime. Review the lifetime as you had before.

After recalling and reviewing your second past lifetime, try reviewing several more lifetimes. If you are having any difficulty with these processes, just keep trying. And if you need to, have somebody else ask you the questions. This will enable you to devote full and complete attention on your recall ability.

## *HYPNOTIC TECHNIQUES & FINGER SIGNALS*

Another tool that you can use are hypnotic finger signals to determine whether you are seeing all there is in the lifetime or incident. Simply tell yourself in your mind to relax. As you relax, tell your unconscious mind that it will communicate directly with your conscious mind via finger signals. Move your left index finger for a "yes" signal and your right index finger for a "no" signal.

Now as you enter into your past life, you can review an incident. Once you view it, you can ask mentally, "Is there anything more that you are not seeing to the incident?" A yes finger signal will tell you that there is something more. You can then ask if the "more" of the incident happened earlier than what you saw or later. Your finger signals will direct you accordingly. You can then ask your unconscious mind to bring you to that point where you are not seeing what happened.

In some cases, the earlier part of the incident isn't actually in the incident but in an earlier lifetime. So you can ask mentally, "Does it take place in an earlier lifetime?" Your finger signals will guide you accordingly.

The following is a transcript of a man I worked with who had an addiction to sex. He was so fixated and obsessed about it that he would spend most of his time daydreaming, visualizing about it. He would buy sexually specific magazines. He would also get involved with women where there was really nothing between himself and the women except the sex. Once the sex was over, he would wonder why he was even with the woman. Of course, the woman would feel used and he would never be satisfied. This caused him to have a trail of broken relationships with no satisfaction.

Here is a transcript of our work together. (Cl = client, R = Rich).

R: Okay, tell me what you would like to work on.

Cl:  I would like to know why I have this sexual attraction to women that I am really not interested in. I have read a bit about sexual addiction, and that fits me pretty well.

R: In what way?

Cl:  Well, I would go after any woman that payed the least attention to me. It was kind of a challenge. But once I got them, that is, had sex with them, I would want to get away from them as soon as possible.

R: How long has this behavior been with you?

Cl: Since I was sixteen years old.

R: All right. Ready?

Cl: Yes!

R: I want you to relax as best as you can. I want you to hear a soft voice in your mind that repeatedly says, "You are relaxing deeper and deeper." Hear that voice now. (He nods his head.) As you hear that voice, you relax deeper and deeper. With each breath you take, you relax even more. (His head falls forward. It is obvious that he is deeply relaxed.) Now, (I reach over and lift his left index finger) a movement of this finger is a "yes" signal. (I reach over and lift his right index finger) a movement of this finger is a "no" signal. Is that acceptable?

Cl: Lifts his left index finger indicating a "yes".

R: You will be able to talk with me. However, if at any point there is any confusion in your conscious awareness, your unconscious mind will take over and give the appropriate finger signals. Is this acceptable?

Cl: Lifts his left index finger indicating a "yes".

R: Now, float up about 500 feet above the earth. Tell me when you are there!

Cl: I'm there!

R: As you descend towards the earth, you will enter into a past life that is the cause for your present life sexual addiction. Tell me when you land.

Cl: I've landed.

R: Look at your feet. What are you wearing?

Cl: I have leather on my feet.

R: Describe yourself.

Cl: I'm a male about 22 years old. I feel like I am some sort of Don Juan. I have many women interested in me. I have sex with them but there is no real love that I feel for them.

R: Anything else?

Cl: Yes. I find myself going earlier to about when I was sixteen. There was a woman that I was deeply in love with. Just being with her satisfied me. But I lost her.

R: How did you lose her?

Cl: That's not clear. I don't see any pictures, but I just know that some man who had money and power wanted her. I think she wanted me. But he forced her into something that she couldn't control. He somehow caused her to die. I just know that she left me due to death.

R: Then what happened?

Cl: Well, after that I never met anyone who filled me so completely. When I came out of my slump, it was like I was looking for her in all my sexual wanderings.

R: You were looking for love or whatever that special feeling was, but couldn't find it?

Cl: Yeah. It was like I knew I would never have all that special feeling again with the loss of her. So I would indulge in women and sex, looking for that feeling.

R: Is there anything more that you are not seeing?

Cl: I don't know. (But as he says that, his left index finger moves indicating a "yes" signal.)

R: Is what you need to see earlier than what you have been seeing?

Cl: Left index finger moves - "yes".

R: Is it in that lifetime?

Cl: Right finger moves - "no".

R: Is it an earlier lifetime?

Cl: Left index finger moves - "yes".

R: Go to that earlier lifetime now and see what remains to be seen.

Cl: Oh. There is a woman I have just met in my present lifetime. I have never felt that way with a woman before. There is a special energy. She understands me and makes me feel in ways that no one before her has. I suddenly had an intuition that this woman is that one I knew in the earlier lifetime. When I move to the earlier lifetime, I see that the woman and I had a special spiritual relationship then. We made a vow to meet each other again. But in that following lifetime, she was taken away from me early.

R: What was the earlier lifetime relationship like?

Cl: We were very spiritual. It seemed like we could do telepathy, know each other's thoughts. Like we were soul mates. It was almost painful to not be with her.

R: How does that seem to you?

Cl: (Smiles) You know I never believed in the theory about soul mates but that is what I have been looking for. Wow. I was looking for love and that feeling of being with someone in that spiritual, special energy way. But the only way, I could get close to that feeling, or at least the only way in which I expressed that was through sex. No wonder I was addicted.

R: Do you realize you said, "Was addicted!"

Cl: (Smiles) Yeah, I just caught it as you said it.

R: Want to find out more about your present life honey?

Cl: Oh yeah.

R: Okay. Back in the earliest lifetime, when you had that spiritual lifetime with the woman. Look at her eyes.

Cl: Okay.

R: Do you know anyone in the present lifetime who has eyes like that?

Cl: Yeah. Her. The one I just met.

R: Anything else?

Cl: Yeah. Most of the women that I would go after, had eyes similar but not the same. I guess I was seeking her out, huh?

R: Maybe! How does your addiction seem to you now?

Cl: Clearer. I know why I do it now. I feel like I have more control over myself and my sexuality now.

### *Comments:*

Could it be possible that all addictions within a person are really a search for a powerful, spiritual energy or beingness that for some reason they can only come close to artificially via drugs, food, alcohol or the like?

In the case above, the man was looking for love but didn't receive it the way in which he wanted. So he substituted sex and passion for love.

Through past life therapy he not only found the underlying reason for his sexual addiction, but he also handled it just by looking at the past life times involved with his addiction.

Notice that the use of finger signals revealed more information faster than before his conscious mind and awareness could. This is because his fingers were directly channeled to the unconscious mind. The unconscious mind could directly reveal information by a finger movement, rather than the slower process of taking unconscious information, presenting it the conscious mind and then saying it with the mouth and vocal cords.

# Chapter 5

## Introduction To Past Life Therapy

Traditional Western medical thought was that all illnesses were organic and totally physical in nature and cause. There was very little that a good shot of penicillin could not cure. Things are different now however.

Recently we have seen the traditional fields of medicine and healing become more tolerant, if not total accepting of some alternative types of healing and therapies, i.e. acupuncture and chiropractic.

With the advances in medicine and the emergence of the wholistic science and health-oriented specialists, illness is finally being put in the spot where it belongs. That is, illness comes from the mind itself. At one time this was considered impossible. Now, with the new research on the mind and altered states of consciousness, it is known that the mind has more control over the body than was ever before assumed.

The traditional medical people will cautiously admit that perhaps 80% of all illnesses are psychosomatically aggravated. Now "psycho" derived from the word "psyche" means "soul" or "mind". "Somatic" comes from "soma" which means thebody. Thus psychosomatic means essentially influence of mind/soul on the physical body.

When psychosomatic is used as in the term psychosomatic illness, it is used to mean that even though the client feels pain and will admit to being ill, there is no organic physical foundation for the illness. This invariably led doctors into trying to outsmart the minds of their patients by prescribing an imaginary drug called a placebo which is usually made up of sugar, for what doctors considered to be an imaginary illness. Gee, sometimes the placebo even seemed to work - but not always.

To the past life therapist however, all illnesses come from the mind. All illnesses are indeed psychosomatic. This should raise perhaps the most important question, "If all illnesses come from the mind, how does it happen?" That is, "how does it occur that the mind can influence the activities of the body in such a way as to cause illness, even death?"

You might remember back from an earlier chapter about the girl on the bike who had an accident and later had severe headaches. We will now explore that same incident but from the following perspective.

When the girl was thrown from the bike, her head hit the street and she went unconscious. At this moment, if a person came up to her and asked her how much 4+4 equals, she would not reply.

_Comment:_ This lack of motion and perceptiveness from the unconscious girl, or anybody who is unconscious for that matter, made medical researchers believe that unconsciousness was total and complete.

This has been proven to be false by patients who underwent surgery. Doctors, while in the midst of an operation, noticed that even though the patient was anaesthesized into unconsciousness, the patient was aware of what was going on. For example, there was a case of a doctor who said aloud that he thought he was losing the patient. Within seconds of the doctor's statement, the patient got worse. It appeared that the patient was listening to the doctor and reacting to him, much like a hypnotized subject responding to the suggestions of the hypnotist.

If the client or the patient was supposedly oblivious to the environment while unconscious and yet capable of responding to the doctors statements, then what part of the mind was listening for the patient to respond to the doctor's statements in the first place?

The answer is the _subconscious mind._

Now to get back to the incident. A crowd begins to gather around the unconscious girl. A woman who knows the girl runs up, sees her lying there and shouts, "Oh my god, is she dead?" Then an ambulance, with the siren blaring approaches the scene. The girl is taken into the ambulance and brought to the hopsital. Outside of the concussion, unconsciousness and shock, she is allright.

Now the girl is a woman at the age of 38; thirty years after the incident, and she is found to suffer from almost constant severe headaches. She goes to the doctor who prescribes medicine but that does not rid the girl of the problem. The doctor advises the girl to have her head X-rayed in order to uncover if there is a tumor or any other abnormal growths that could be the cause of the headache. But nothing is discovered.

The doctor states that the headaches must be psychosomatic as there are no organic reasons that have been found to be the source of the headaches. And for the most part, that is as far as the healing can go. Perhaps the severe headaches can be placed under control by medicine and drugs but the cause cannot be found.

A past life therapist who understands the connection between illness and the mind would realize that some incident had to have occurred for the woman to be having the headaches now. But how are these two separate incidents - being hit on the bicycle as a little girl and the severe headaches as a grown woman, related?

### *TRIGGERS - THE CONNECTING FACTOR*

The connecting factor is that somewhere in the present time environment there exists a factor which is attached to an earlier incident. I call this factor a trigger. It is the trigger in the present environment that calls up the incident which occurred earlier and presents that early incident to the present time mind complete with all the pain and sensations that were originally present in the first incident.

A trigger in the case mentioned above is the sound of a siren. The woman walks down the street and hears the sirens of a fire engine or ambulance go by. The sirens are a factor that were present in the original incident. Her unconscious mind upon hearing the blare of the sirens in present time instantaneously makes a search in the memory for other incidents containing sirens and the sound they make. The one to become reawakened was the original incident containing the bicycle accident. All the pain and sensations turn on.

*NOTE:* In many cases, a trigger (such as the blaring siren) can cause an immediate response such as the headache. In some cases however, there can be a delayed response. For example, the siren blare goes by at 12:15pm; then at 2:00pm the headache is just starting. But be assured, the triggers are consistent and real. It was a trigger that got activated, that caused a quiet man to take a gun, enter a MacDonald's in California and shoot over a dozen people.

Regarding the incident above, other triggers could be:

1) moving so fast that the environment becomes a blur - she was thrown through the air from the bicycle

2 ) surrounded by large groups of people - she was surrounded by people.

3) a woman's voice either saying, "Oh my God, is she dead?" or maybe just the pitch and tone of a voice that is similar to the voicein the original incident.

4) the smell of burnt rubber, the sound of tires skidding and many other subtle elements that were in the original incident.

Very powerful triggers are created when the conscious mind is not available to analyze those triggers. In the example above, the girl developed powerful triggers that she did not know of because they became triggers while she was unconscious and unaware.

## *HOW THE CONSCIOUS MIND IS MADE UNCONSCIOUS*

There are four ways in which the conscious mind can be put out of action:

1) drugs

2) hypnosis

3) Intense pain (usually leading to unconsciousness).

4) Implants - Special Energy Forces

When any one of the four factors is present and applied with force or intensity, the conscious mind goes unconscious and dormant. This is similar to a person who undergoes great stress and pain. Usually they will be in shock. The shock occurs because the senses are overwhelmed. This causes the conscious mind to go unconscious.

While the conscious mind is idle (knocked out), the subconscious mind takes control and is given free reign. It becomes something of a mad photographer taking pictures of everything; sometimes out of focus; other times out of perspective. However, with the subconscious mind in control, it will record pictures, sounds, and statements, that for the most part will be very difficult to recollect or remember in conscious mind awareness.

During periods of unconsciousness, the analytical conscious mind is dormant and does not keep tabs or a central filing on what the subconscious mind is recording. Then when the conscious mind comes to, it begins to take over from where it left off, that is from just before it became unconscious. This means that the whole period of unconsciousness now contains a very precise and clear record of all that happened while it was unconscious. The only problem is that the conscious mind does not even know that this data even exists. It is this hidden data that is out of the reach of the conscious mind that allows the triggers to come into existence and cause pain, illnesse and discomfort.

## PAST LIFE THERAPY FOR THE RELEASE OF PHOBIA

This case deals with a woman I worked with in Washington, D.C. back in the 1970's. She was a lawyer and had a tremendous fear of feathers. During summer days, she could not picnic on the grassy spots like everyone else, because inevitably a pigeon would land looking for a handout. Madelyn would become so frightened by the feathers (not the bird) that she would have to get up and run away.

When she came to me as a client, she was about 31 years old. During our first session she mentioned that she was afraid of feathers. She had this fear from a very early age.

Madelyn told me that she was about five years old when her mother tried to get her to overcome her fear. Her mother took a feather from a toy Indian chief's headdress and approached Madelyn trying to get her to touch it. The mother believed that by getting Madelyn to touch the feather directly, Madelyn would overcome the fear of feathers. According to Madelyn, when she saw her mother approaching with a feather in her hand, Madelyn started shaking and went into convulsions.

Madelyn never overcome her fear and in fact, when she walked down the street, if a pigeon came near to her, she would duck into the nearest store and stay there until the pigeon went away.

She mentioned that it was not the pigeon, but rather the feathers that scared her. Picnics were absolutely out of the question, because there would always be at least one type of bird or another around. At the sight of a pigeon, she would toss her sandwich into her lunch bag, running for the nearest shelter from the bird. When she entered a supermarket, she could not walk down the aisle where they stocked feather dusters. (*The trigger for Madelyn's fear was obviously feathers.*)

I worked with her to bring her to the memory of the past life or lives (See How To Run Past Lives) that was involved behind the fear of feathers. I had her rise up 500 hundred feet into the air as you learned to do earlier. I told her to descend into the past life that contained the original incident that causes her present time fear of feathers. She landed into the past life.

Madelyn remembered being back in an early American Indian tribe. She was a young male about 19 years of age. Her tribe was fighting another tribe. As she recalled the incident, she saw that her past life body had been pierced in the chest and heart with a spear by her enemy. Just before death ensued, he (Madelyn) saw the chief of the other tribe on his horse wearing a long feathered headdress and supervising the battle.

After she reviewed the incident a few times, she noticed that she felt pounds lighter. Other sensations she experienced were those of lightheadedness, buzzing, and tingling throughout her body. She felt that something had 'released' the fear of feathers.

About three weeks later I received a letter from her stating "imagine my delight when I went into a millinery store and got fitted for a feathered hat." The fear of feathers came to an end and never returned. But it ended only after she reviewed the original incident that put the fear of feathers into her mind in the first place.

The reason for the fear of feathers was that on a subconscious level, she equated the feathers with death. After all, that was the last thing she saw before the death of the body.

## *WHY PEOPLE DON'T REMEMBER PAST LIVES*

At this point I would like to to answer one of the most often asked questions: If past lives are real, how come more people do not remember them?

Some skeptics have claimed that since people do not remember past lives, there cannot be past lives. This assumption is erroneous for two reasons. First, there are many people who have remembered past lives. But who can they tell or talk to about these memories? Chances are for the most part, these people keep themselves hidden and in the closet so to speak to avoid insult and in validation from others. Second, what about people who cannot remember what happened during their first or second birthdays? Does this mean that they did not exist when they were one of two because they cannot remember what happened then? The real situation around past lives is that for one reason or another they remain hidden to the conscious mind until the proper steps are taken to bring these memories forward to the conscious mind.

Answer the next 2 questions honestly and you will understand the number one reason why people do not remember past lives:

A) List 10 things that you would not mind remembering:

1.

2.

3.

4.

5.

6.

7.

8.

9.

10.

B) Now list 10 things that you would not mind forgetting:

1.

2.

3.

4.

5.

6.

7.

8.

9.

10.

You will probably notice that those things that you listed that you would not mind remembering are pleasant things. Things that you enjoyed or loved. You will also notice that the things that you would not mind forgetting are those things that are physically or emotionally painful. In other words, the mind tries to protect you by having you forget the unpleasant and painful experiences.

One very important law to do with past life therapy is that only the past lives that contain pain, hypnosis, implants and/or drugs, are the ones that are the source or cause for illness. Pleasant memories do not cause illness. Negative memories do. People become ill and stay ill because they do not want to recall negative incidents. They think that if they recall the past negative incident, that all the bad from that incident will turn on totally. What they do not realize is that it is the non-confront attitude that they hold which causes the problems. To put it simply, past life incidents lose their effect on a person's health, well being and so on by simply reviewing that past life.

This theory of reviewing a past incident is not new. It is the basis by which most psychologists and psychiatrists work with their patients. The fundamental difference however is that they do not go back far enough to handle the problems. Going to five years old in a person's present life is good if the original problem or incident begins there. However, the problem may actually have its source in an event that may have occurred millions of years earlier. So as you learn to go back into past lives you must realize that an event has occurred containing pain, drugs, hypnosis, and/or implants that is now creating negative effects in the present.

Some people are frightened that they will remember not being nice in past lives. Chances are that nobody was ever nice all the time. Consider that within our own 3,000 years of recorded history on earth, we have had murder, killing, and pestilence. The important thing to realize is that you are here in the present time. You are simply going back into memory banks to clear up some issues that are causing you to not be fully yourself now in the present. Seeing yourself as a negative personality does not mean that you will suddenly become negative. In fact, by seeing the negative personality you actually stop yourself from becoming negative.

And just the opposite can happen as well. Some people might wish to work with past lives but more as a means of an escape from their lives. Somebody who feels insignificant in their present life suddenly remembers being Napoleon. The past life therapist must always be on the alert for such people.

## STORED ENERGY CHARGE

When you view an incident, you discharge its stored energy charge. This is how the incident becomes released. By "released" I mean that the past life incident is erased and all the influence that it exerted on the present life ceases. By "stored energy charge" I mean the following: each incident, especially that of a negative, painful or unconscious element, contains within it a charge of energy which I call the Life Force Energy. This Life Force Energy then affects the body causing the body to react in the manner already dictated by what is recorded in the imagery of the subconsciously recorded event.

This stored charge of energy is similar in electronics to a capacitor. A capacitor, in electronics terms, is a device which stores an electrical charge or voltage for an extended amount of time depending on the parameters of the capacitor.

Now the energy charge contained in a lifetime memory makes the mind and body respond and react for good or bad depending on the incident that manifested the chardged energy in the first place.

So then the grand purpose of past life recall therapy is not to indulge in the ego or run away from ones responsibility in the present, but rather to release the 'charged energy' from the incident. This release causes the stored charge to diminish and finally release. At that time of full release there will be no more stored energy to cause illness.

Let us move onto Chapter 6 where we will learn to employ past life therapy.

# C h a p t e r 6

## Past Life Therapy Methods

Past life therapy methods are similar to past life recall methods. The difference is in the method used once inside the past life event that causes the present life problem. In past life therapy, you don't need to recall the entire lifetime, only the entire incident that causes the present time pattern, behavior, or difficulty.

*NOTE:* I address these techniques as if you are using them with a client. However, you can easily use these methods for yourself as well.

### PLT METHOD #1

Most of the time, any past life event that causes present life difficulties can be flushed out of the unconscious mind and brought to conscious awareness by a statement or phrase that was said or thought during the original incident. This statement or thought becomes a hypnotic command to the person even today.

Here is an example of a client I worked with over ten years ago. This was his problem.

My client, Bob, owned a family business that had been in operation for three generations. He was the sole owner. Within a certain time period, he realized that he was losing several business clients that had been clients of his family business from the very beginning.

Bob went into panic and depression.

Bob entered my office and sat down. I asked him what was going on. Here is a transcript of what happened in our session.


R: Well, what can I do for you today?

Bob: I'm here because I'm worried about my business. Many of the clients that were with the business when my father and my grandfather ran the business are leaving me now. A couple of them called and said they were going to order their parts from some other company. It's only a matter of time before the other clients cancel their orders and my business goes under.

R: Have you done anything to try to change the course of events that your business is going through?

Bob: Yeah. I had an appointment with a woman who has an

M.B.A. (At this point, his face flushes, his breathing gets heavy. He is distinctly uncomfortable)

R: I guess so! So what came out of that meeting?

Bob: Well, at one point during the meeting I lost my breath. I felt an intense pain in my stomach. I saw black in front of my eyes. I started to perspire. I couldn't stand being there!

R: Anything else?

Bob: Yeah. I got this thought in my mind, "I need someone to save my ass!" (As he said that statement, he became even redder in the face.)

R: How do you feel now?

Bob: I feel exactly the same now as I felt during the lunch with the MBA person.

R: Any reason why?

Bob: Yeah! Because I'm coming to you to save my ass!

R: Ready to handle this?

Bob: Sure...

R: I want you to notice the feelings that you have in your body. At the same time, I want you to say out loud, "I need someone to save my ass!"

Bob: (Silence) I can't say it. (He stutters and his face turns very red).

R: Okay! Mentally say it to yourself.

Bob: Okay..

R: Now let yourself look at any images or pictures that suddenly enter your awareness. Tell me about them!

Bob: It's the time of the Roman empire. I see gladiators fighting.

R: Look at yourself. How are you dressed? What are you wearing?

Bob: I don't know. This is foolish. I like to watch gladiator shows on television. That's all this is. It's something I've seen on TV.

R: Just humor me and go on with this, okay? (He nods) Go to the time when you think, "I need someone to save my ass!" Repeat it. Now what happens?

Bob: Oh! (Looks like he had some sort of insight or cognition.) I am dressed in robes. I'm a Christian and I'm in the coliseum. I'm expected to fight the huge gladiators.

R: What happens next?

Bob: I know that *I need someone to save my ass!* I pray to Jesus that he will come and save me from the gladiators. They give me a sword and I go out into the coliseum. I see a gladiator coming at me with a sword.

R: What happens now?

Bob: I drop my sword. The gladiator just comes up to me and sticks his sword into my stomach. There is *blackness*. I can only see darkness. The pain in my stomach is intense. I can hardly breathe. I am perspiring. I can't stand. I fall to the ground and die.

R: Return to the beginning of the incident. (He nods.) Okay, rerun the event silently from beginning to the end. (He does so.) How do you feel now?

Bob: I feel relieved. (His breathing was back to normal, perspiration stopped. He felt good all over. I feel lighter as if something has lifted off of my shoulders).

R: Okay. Now rerun the life time incident three more times.

Each time you go through it I want you to look for more detail than you have seen yet. (He nods to me that he has done this.) Is there anything about this incident that remains hidden or that you should see but haven't?

Bob: Nods his head "No". I have seen what I needed to see.

R: Try this. Say out loud, "I need someone to save my ass!"

Bob: "I need someone to save my ass!" That's pretty silly. (He smiles.)

R: Remember when you couldn't even say that just a few minutes ago?

Bob: Yeah. That's strange!

R: How do you feel about your business now?

Bob: Well, I don't need someone to save my ass anymore. I'll make my business work.

### Comments :

Notice that the client comes to me and the very language that he uses is descriptive -- literally descriptive and not just metaphorically. **The very words he used to describe what is going on now, are the actual words used in the past life incident.**

Notice that the client responded physically to the thought of his loss of the business and the hiring of the M.B.A. in the very way, and with those specific feeeelings and reactions, that he experienced while dying in the Roman past life. The client did nothing more than demonstrate those specific actions, feelings and thoughts that were contained in the past life.

At the time of entering the coliseum arena, he believed that Jesus or some other such spiritual being would come down and save him from the disaster about to befall him. Hence the thought, "I need some one to save my ass." In addition, the sword was thrust inside him in the stomach area causing pain which he complained about. Further, he saw a darkness in front of his face. Plus the other manifestations such as perspiration, breathlessness, and the inability to stand up.

Why would this person go back to the Roman coliseum time incident? Because we were specifically looking for a lifetime in which those specific feelings and thoughts were present. In doing this, the unconscious mind can specifically locate the past lives pertinent to the present life problem. These past lives will contain all the factors, i.e., perspiration, unconsciousness, fear, even the same wording ("I need someone to save my ass!").

This is much like a computer program where even if you lose the name of the file of data that you want to access, you can enter in details of what should be in that past life incident and the unconscious mind can return to the past memory and find that specific lifetime and the information contained in it.

So then, one way to trace out a past life experience is to find the statement or statements (the mental thoughts or internal voice that always accompanies such an incident ) that the person experiences or is aware of when in the present life, and use that as a reference point to enter into a past lifetime.

Bob's gladiator lifetime was the primary lifetime that caused his present problems. How do we know that? First, a primary incident must contain force. Either you're doing something to somebody or they are doing something to you. But in that force there must be pain, unconsciousness (lack of awareness), hypnosis, drugs/poisons, or death. This Roman lifetime contained the pain, force, unconsciousness and death that makes it a primary incident. In addition, with the release of the incident, his present life behavior and responses no longer existed. This indicates that this was a primary lifetime incident.

The only therapy needed here or for any part of past life therapy is to get the conscious mind to become aware of the pictures and images and feelings and thoughts/internal voices stored in the subconscious mind. The past life scenarios will repeat themselves over and over again until such time as you make them conscious by putting your awareness on them. Once you have done this you have released the incident from ever influencing and affecting you again.

## *PLT METHOD #2*

This second method is works well with most people. It requires no elicitation of feelings, thoughts or pictures. In this case, you ask the person to imagine himself growing inches above his head. Next have the client imagine that he is extending his feet several inches below his feet. Now have the client imagine himself to be hundreds of feet above the ground, hovering in the sky.

Next tell the client, that as he descends toward the earth, he will enter into the past life that is the cause for his present time problem(s).

Usually, at that point the client will come down to earth on his own and be inside of the past life that causes the present time problem. Below is a transcript using this method.

R: What would you like to work on?

CL: I have a difficult relationship with my boss. He is always down my throat. I get so stressed out that I eat more than I should.

R: So what do you want past life therapy to do for you?

CL: I want to know where I knew this man before. Maybe this will help me to understand why I have this relationship with him.

R: Okay. Imagine your head stretching inches above your head. Nod when you do this. (The client nods.) Now imagine your feet stretching inches below the soles of your feet. Nod when you do this. (Client nods.) All right, now imagine yourself hundreds of feet up in the air. Nod when you do this. (Client nods.) Now look down at the neighborhood. I want you to start to descend towards the earth. As you descend you will enter into the past life that is the cause of your present time relationship, the way it is, with your boss. Nod your head when you touch down on the ground. Client nods her head. Now that you have touched down into the lifetime that is the cause for your present time life problem with your boss, I want you to describe your surroundings.

CL: I'm out in a field. It's daytime.

R: Are you male or female?

CL: Female

R: About how old are you at this time?

CL: About 18 years old.

R: Has the event that causes your present time problem happened yet or is it still to happen?

CL: It hasn't happened yet.

R: Okay then, move forward until you are at the beginning of the event.

CL: I am at a table and I am with a man who is dressed in a military uniform. He is telling me that I am not good enough and that he is leaving me. He has been with other women.

R: Military uniform? What type of uniform and when does when does this happen?

CL: It's during the civil war.

R: What happens next?

CL: He leaves me to go to war. I hear that he was killed in the war.

R: How do you feel about that?

CL: I don't mind. I don't feel anything for him.

R: Okay. Is that the incident? Is there anything further that you should see?

CL: I don't think so.

R: How do you feel about your boss now?

CL: It's still there. The feeling is still there.

_NOTE:_ This tells me that we did not hit the important incident. So notice what I do next.

R: Is there an earlier lifetime involved? Does the reason for your present time relationship with your boss come from an earlier life?

CL: I think so.

R: All right. Go up 500 feet into the air. Tell me when you are there.

CL: Now.

R: All right, this time I want you to descend towards the earth. When you land, I want you to return to the past life time that contains the event that causes your present time problem relationship with your boss. Tell me when you land!

CL: (says nothing)

R: What is happening?

CL: I can't return to the earth. I can't come down.

R: All right then, let your self come down into the life time that has the event that is the problem your present time problem.

CL: I have landed. I am back into that past life of the Civil War. I am in a field. But a man in a military suit on a horse races down the hill towards me.

R: Is that the same man who left you to go to war?

CL: No. It's a different person. He rides by and attacks me. I fall to the ground and he tries to rape me. He is forcing me down, taking my clothes off. He finishes with me and as he lays down I reach for a knife that he had. He starts to get up. I stab him in the back several times until he is dead.

R: Look at his eyes. Do they remind you of anybody you know now?

CL: Yes. My boss.

R: Run the incident again seeing it from beginning to end. How do you feel about your boss now?

CL: I am angry.

R: Towards your boss?

CL: No. Towards men.

*Note:* Notice how the issue was about her boss. But once the incident was reviewed and released, the issue really came to her basic issue which is that of men in general, rather than in specific. So to handle this, I now look for the incident that causes this feeling and response to all men inside of her.

R: Let's go to the primary lifetime that contains the primary incident for why you are angry towards men. Go up 500 feet in the air. Tell me when you are there. (Client responds affirmatively.) Now let yourself descend to the earth. When you land you will be back in the lifetime that contains the primary incident for the anger towards men. Tell me when you land.

CL: I have landed. I am in a cave with my tribe. I am a woman.

R: Move to the beginning of the incident and run the event.

CL: I am in a cave with my tribe. Men from some other tribe attack and enter our cave. One of the men comes for me. I pick up a spear and kill him. The men left the cave.

R: Run the incident one more time silently from the start to finish. (Client nods her head indicating that she has done so.) How do you feel towards men now?

CL: The anger is gone. It seems that in each life when a man transgressed me or my territory I ended up doing him in. The situation is different now. I feel different. I feel lighter and more relaxed.

R: How do you feel about your boss now?

CL: Makes a gesture with her face and eyes as if she doesn't care at all. He doesn't bother me now.


## *PLT METHOD #3*

A third method for reviewing past lives is to create a movie screen. And as the person is seated in front of the movie screen, he is to see his past life. This has several advantages to it.

The first is that you are in a dissociated state. By seeing the past life on the movie screen, you are seeing it as an outside director rather than as a player in the part. Should some part of the memory of the past life have a negative or difficult event in it, it will have less of an impact and even less of an effect. And due to this the client would be able to see the event easily and without discomfort.

Have the client review the "movie" on the screen several times. At the end of the movie, have the client step into the past life. By reliving the incident in the associated, physical kinesthetic channels of the body, the past life incident discharges.

## POINTS TO REMEMBER

•When it comes to past lives, no matter what you do, or no matter what technique you use to do it, the only important thing is to get the conscious awareness involved and have it review the past life. This releases the past life.

• Past Life Therapy is not dangerous - you are only remembering deep memory incidents.

# Chapter 7

## Checking Your Work

Whenever I work with a client I always want to test my work to make sure that it has been effective and that it is already working. I do this by putting the client into an imaginary time machine, send the client into the future and have him watch himself in the old situation but with the new changes instead of the old behavior. At that point, I (and the client) know that the PLT session has worked.

A wonderful story that I use frequently in my seminars and writings has to do with a study that was done on visualization. Three basketball teams were established at a university. One team, the control team was to practice several hours a day. As the control team, their practice was do nothing but be on the basketball court. The second team was to practice their shots physically while on the basketball court. The third team was to practice their shots from the court but only in their minds. They would visualize that they were making their shots only.

After a specified test time, the results were tabulated. The control team that never practiced did not improve. The team that practiced their shots physically improved on the order of about 27 percent better. The team that simply visualized improved on the order of about 28 percent.

**The results indicated to the researchers that there is no difference between an imagined reality and an actually experienced reality.** The team that visualized scored better since in their minds, they would visualize that each shot that they made was a successful scoring shot. (After all, who would want to visualize that they missed?)

Since to the brain, there is no difference between an actually experienced experience and an imagined experience, this provides an easy way to test your work. The best test of your work is time alteration.

### *TIME ALTERATION*

Let's suppose that you have just worked with a person who has a fear of elevators. You have done your past life regression work expertly and the client has shown a radical change in her reaction to the use of elevators. So how do you know that this will stand up under test?

One way is to have her go into an elevator immediately. Perhaps there is a building nearby that has an elevator. Direct your client to that building and have her go up and down that elevator to different floors, to the top and back down several times. Have the client do it by herself; with no support team or person.

Sometimes, however, immediate tests are not feasible. For instance, if I remedy a person's fear of airplanes, it may not be easy to just have a person book a flight to somewhere in order to test the fear. When immediate tests of your work are not feasible or possible, use time alteration to test your work.

### *CHANGING TIME*

Since the brain does not know the difference between an actually experienced experience and an imagined experience, if someone were to imagine themselves in the future, a part of his consciousness would be in that imagined future.

So then, by asking someone to imagine himself in a specified time in the future, in a specified place, doing a specified action, the brain and awareness actually conceives itself to be at that place and time doing that specified action.

When immediate testing is not possible, this is what you can do to test your work. Have the client imagine himself being in the very situation or environment with which he is having difficulty. Do this both before and after your past life therapy work. You will observe that your client has changed his reactions and responses to his problems. Usually, the problem is no longer! (Of course if you are doing this PLT work on yourself, you test your work by doing the same as you would for a client.)

For example, a woman I worked with had terrible difficulties with her boss that led to stress and overeating on her part. I tested her responses through time alteration. That is, I had her imagine that she was at work and dealing with her boss. Now, here she was sitting in my office. Her boss was nowhere near the place. I asked her to think of her boss and imagine that she was in his office. Immediately, her face reddened, she clenched her hands, her jaw closed tight, many parts of her body tightened up. All this over an hallucination. You see, her brain did not know the difference whether she was in my office or his office, because once you feed the brain the triggers it needs,  it takes over from there. The very act of her getting tight and tense, indicates of course, what she does with her body when she is with her boss.

After we finishedthe Past Life Therapy session, I tested the therapeutic impact by asking her to imagine that she is in her boss' office once again. If I do not see the same body responses - tightening of muscles and the like, then I know that a change has taken place. If I do notice the same old body and mind responses, then my work has not taken effect and needs to be done again.

Another way in which you can use time alteration to test your work, is to have the client move into the future where he is once again in the same environment, with the same person or persons, and the like, where he experiences his problems. Then have him run through the situation, - associated (as if he is actually there and not watching himself on a movie screen ) - and tell you what he does and feels automatically, moment by moment!

Most importantly, if there is a change in the way that the person acts and reacts to the problem (or people or environment in that problem) even though they are seated in your office, you have made a therapeutic impact on the client.

A hidden benefit of time alteration (having your client imagine himself in the future with the new changes) is that you actually trigger the client to respond in the improved and desired ways whenever the client is in that environment or with those people who give him the difficult times.

### *TRIGGERS*

Triggers are any factors, that when perceived, set off a cetain behavior or state of mind or body. For example, you go to talk to someoneand he abruptly turns his back on you. You will most likely react to that trigger with anger or confusion.

To understand this concept of triggers do the following:

1) say the word "pen".

2) as you say the word "pen" think of a white, puffy cloud.

3) do this five times.

Now say the word "pen" and notice what happens. You may notice that you get a picture of a pen but you will also notice that you now get the picture of the white, billowy cloud as well. "Pen" has become associated with cloud.

This same situation applies to the client. If you have the client run through a future event where he is different, say in the work environment, and shows the favorable qualities he wants to in that environment, then you are actually reinforcing him to become that way and show those qualities when he is in the work environment. Time alteration of the future actually triggers a person to become that way when he is in that environment or with that person.

# Chapter 8

## Accessing New Behaviors
## Talents and Resources with PLT

In much of the literature about past life recall and therapy, no one seems to understand that past life recall and therapy goes beyond handling problems and illnesses. One such 'beyond' for past life therapy and recall is the ability to regain and manifest abilities and talents that you once possessed.

For instance, John wants to be better at handling himself in front of groups. He wants to give lectures and seminars to groups of people. Yet he finds himself afraid and nervous to do so. Below is the script of my session with him and how we handled not only his fear and nervousness of public speaking but also how we helped him gain his ability to speak in public.

Richard: What can I help you with, John?

John: I want to be able to talk to people in groups and seminars. I want to overcome my fear of talking to groups of people. But I also want to be able to give dynamic lectures and seminars as well.

Richard: All right, let's see what we can do! John, I want you to imagine yourself rising up about 500 feet into the air. Tell me when you can do that.

John: (closing his eyes) Okay, I am in the air.

Richard: Now start to descend towards the earth. As you descend, you will go back into the past life that is the cause for your present time difficulty with group lectures and speaking. Tell me when you land.

John: I have landed.

Richard: Describe to me where you are.

John: I am in Greece. I'm wearing a toga and sandals. There is a large audience. They seem to have come out to see and hear me speak.

Richard: Has the incident that causes you your present time problems already happened or yet to happen?

John: It's just about to happen.

Richard: Continue. What happens next?

John: I am a well known speaker. I can't get my name, but people have come to hear me speak. There is something wrong though. There is a different type of energy around. Something is going to happen.

Richard: Continue.

John: I get out on to the stage. I start to speak. I seem to be talking about the government and people in the government.

Richard: Continue.

John: Suddenly, as if on cue, several men jump up on the stage on both sides of the stage. They are carrying sticks and clubs. They start to hit me on the head and face and then they hit me all over the body. They keep hitting me. I go unconscious, fall to the ground. HMMMMM.

Richard: Anything else?

John: Yeah. They killed my body.

Richard: Did anybody try to help you?

John: No. Either no one wanted to help me or they were too confused to do anything.

Richard: Rerun the entire incident from beginning to end. Notice the details.

John: The men who killed me were put up to it by the very people that I was going to talk out about and expose. They warned me not to talk about those topics. I had the choice not to say anything. And I probably would have lived. But I couldn't do that. I felt that people needed to know whatever it was that I knew.

Richard: How does the incident seem to you now?

John: Released.

Richard: Notice how that lifetime influences the present life time.

John: Yeah. I already did that. When I get up in front of people, I'm afraid that they are going to not like what I am saying or not accept me and get up and confront me.

Richard: How do you feel about going out and doing public

speaking and seminars now?

John: I'm ready. I can't wait.

Richard: Good. Now let's see if we can get you back your charisma and public speaking skill that you possessed as that Greek.

John: Okay.

Richard: Go back into that life time and watch yourself at another earlier time when you gave such eloquent and powerful speeches that you made a name for yourself.

John: (Closes his eyes). Yeah. I can see one.

Richard: Notice how you, as the Greek, held yourself. That is how you held your body. Did you stand up straight, at and angle? How did you move your arms and your eyes. Notice your breathing.

John: Yeah. I got that.

Richard: Good. Now transfer those body representations to your present physical body. In other words, hold your body now exactly as you did then.

John: (takes a deep breath) All right.

Richard: Now, notice how you talked. Did you speak loud, soft or a combination? Notice, how did you move your eyes as you talked?

John: I got that.

Richard: Finally, notice what kind of thoughts, what mental state were you in when you were in front of people making your speech.

John: Okay.

Richard: Now transfer all those qualities to your present life body as well.

John: Got it.

Richard: How do you feel about making speeches and public talks now?

John: Wow. I feel great. I understand now how to make that contact with people that makes an effective speech or seminar. This is incredible.

Richard: It sure is! Now see yourself at some time in the future when you are giving a speech or seminar. How do you do?

John: Better than ever. I really can be the great speech giver that I want to be.

## COMMENTS:

The fact is that within all people there is a powerful and elegant behavior by which people can do things. Usually however, there are also negative patterns, which is what most people display. In the case of John, he was displaying a negative internal behavior that resulted in his inability to handle public speaking or seminars. But there was also a powerful model of what he could be in his unconscious mind. All that was needed was to substitute what he had been doing in this present lifetime and replace it with his past life powerful and elegant model.

This replacement of his present life model with his more elegant past life model was done by simply having him imitate the way that he was in the Greek lifetime. By having John assume the same physical characteristics -- body posture, breathing, movement -- and by assuming the same mental state and the same voice characteristics and speed and tone, he, to all intents and purposes, became that Greek orator. In this way he actually assumed the abilities and talents of that past life entity that was in his consciousness and made him want to be a public orator but had brought along the negatives of public orating as well (orating can make you enemies and get you killed!).

A question that is usually asked by my students and clients is, "What if I don't have a past life that has a positive elegant model?" First of all, this is highly unlikely. When it comes to past lives, you usually have at least one -- usually several -- lifetimes filled with an elegant, powerful, positive model.

## *SESSION #2 - - ACCESSING THE PAINTER WITHIN*

A friend confided in me once that he felt that he should be able to paint but that he wasn't fully motivated to do so. He was not motivated because he did not "know what to do" in order to paint. This desire implied to me that he had at least one lifetime when he was an artist. All that was necessary then was to get him back into the past life where he was an artist and have him reestablish his artistic skills.

R: Ready to become an artist?

Cl: (Laughing) Oh yeah!

R: Rise up 500 feet in the air and tell me when you are there.

Cl: Okay.

R: Start to descend towards the earth. When you land, I want you to land in the past lifetime where you were an elegant artist.

Cl: I've landed.

R: Look around and tell me what you see.

Cl: I see a man dressed in clothing of about the time of the renaissance. He is holding several canvasses under his arm and he is walking very fast.

R: Follow him. Where does he go?

Cl: He is going into his art studio.

R: Now, move to when he is actually painting.

Cl: Uh huh. I'm painting now.

R: Watch the way the artist holds himself. The stance and posture of his body. Notice his breathing. Notice how he holds his eyes. Get everything that you can from his physical body and transfer it to your present time body now.

Cl: (After a few moments) Okay. Got it.

R: Now float up and go inside that past life artist body. Look out through his eyes and see what he sees. Think what he thinks. Notice the way in which his mind works. Notice any pictures and images and the like.

Cl: Hmm. Okay.

R: Now bring that mental state of that past life artist into your present life now.

Cl: Okay.

R: Come back to present life and normal awareness but maintain the artist characteristics and qualities.

Cl: (opens his eyes and yawns)

R: How do you feel?

Cl: Great!

R: And what about art and painting now?

Cl: I really feel like I can do it. I'm going to start in the next day or two.

### *Comments:*

The client in this case, stayed in a detached disassociated state of mind as he watched the past life. This is the reason why he talked about that past life personality as "he" instead of "I".

If there are past life models that you want to bring into the present from past lives, the trick is to assume the same physical posture as you did back then. This physical posturing (including breathing, eye movements, etc.) sends signals to your consciousness to "turn on" those past skills and qualities. Next, you should "go inside" that past life body and look out through its eyes. As you do this, you can also turn on the way that you thought and the mental processes that you used when you were at that past life. The final step is to bring the physical characteristics and the mental characteristics back to the present time body and consciousness. At that point, you have brought the skills and abilities back to the present.

You can now test your work by noticing how you feel about the topic now, how you handle the topic now, and so on. You should notice that you now have new resources and skills that are usable right now in present time.

# Chapter 9

## Overcoming Pain with PLT

Pain is the greatest one of the top five afflictions of man. But it should be understood that pain comes from your brain and mind - and not the body itself. Since all pain comes from the mind, it is feasible that pain can be controlled by controlling the mind.

Past life therapy is one of the speediest and most effective technologies for reducing pain -- if not eradicating it completely. One such example of this pain eradication involves tooth aches. In my practice of PLT, I have dealt with many people who were suffering with tooth pain. After only one session of PLT, most clients found that their mouth and teeth pains disappeared immediately once they saw the past life involved with the present life time pain.

## *THE PURPOSE OF PAIN*

In my work through the years, I have discovered that pain is really a communication. It is the unconscious mind striving to communicate an important message to the conscious mind of the person so afflicted.

The reason why the unconscious mind doesn't "get through" to the conscious mind is that they work in dissimilar ways. The conscious mind being analytical and direct, only needs to be told directly. It wants to know - period. The unconscious mind however doesn't think and act linearly but rather in a circular type of thinking.

Dreams are only one of the ways in which the unconscious mind communicates. Yet, how many times have we had earth-shattering dreams only to not be able to understand or interpret them? Interesting as well is the fact that you bring your dream to several experts for analysis and they will all tell you dissimilar things.

The conscious mind wants to know outright and practically screams to the unconscious mind, "Can't you just tell me? Why do I have to go through all this dream stuff and images? I can't interpret what you are trying to tell me!"

So then, conscious mind and unconscious mind break down in communication. The unconscious mind tries to tell what is on it's mind, but the conscious mind doesn't know how to interpret that information. Now let's say that the unconscious mind, which is infinitely more aware than the conscious mind, knows of a condition in the mind and/or body that it wants corrected. The conscious mind gets various different types of communications from the unconscious mind such as dreams, images, fantasies and the like, but still neglects what the unconscious mind is trying to say. The only thing left, the only communication that the unconscious mind can give in order to get the conscious mind's attention is pain.

**All pain is simply a communication of something the unconscious mind wants but which is going unheeded and unfulfilled by the conscious mind.**

For instance, a woman has the inability to speak up for herself in a relationship. And yet speaking up for herself is vital from the unconscious mind's point of view. So what might the unconscious mind do to get her attention, since she most likely disregarded all other attempts at communication by the unconscious mind? How about pain or disease of the mouth, throat, gums and/or teeth? Certainly the pain cannot be ignored. Most likely however, she will go to a dentist, a little novacaine, a little drilling and then, back to normal. You really think so? She still hasn't dealt with the initial problem - her inability to speak up for herself in the relationship.

The unconscious mind thwarted at the first attempt, might then find other areas of the body to affect with pain as well. For instance, sexuality is a form of communication as well. Maybe the lower stomach and sexual organs become diseased or stressed in some way. The bottom line is that the unconscious mind is trying to serve and protect and inform. Until that is done, the person is never really cured or healed.

Where does the unconscious mind get its information -- it's patterns to know what to influence or not? Past lives of course. Here's how it works:

The woman mentioned above, has the problems as stated. She

goes into a past life and discovers that she once talked back to someone in the act of sticking up for herself. The other person used force against her in retaliation for her communication. She was hit on the side of the face, removing a tooth or two and shattering some others. The pain was intense.

Now in this lifetime, (before using PLT) the woman didn't speak up for herself because she remembers at the unconscious level what happened at that time. And the reasoning is that to stick up for oneself is to face confrontation, force, and pain. That's the way it happened in the earlier lifetime. The unconscious mind prompts her to deal with this situation by turning on the pain from that earlier lifetime. Now she has to deal with the fact that she has to stick up for herself and say what she really means and feels, or suffer the pain.

If she is fortunate enough to be aware of past life therapy, she will go back to the lifetime. The viewing of that painful lifetime incident will clear up this lifetime problem. The pain will go away, and she will recognize at the conscious mind awareness that she can confront others and handle her life. Just because in one life, she may have been made to suffer for standing up for her own interests, doesn't mean that it will happen now in this present lifetime. The outcome is that she will now do what her unconscious mind has been prompting her to do for quite some time -- speak up and speak out.

The unconscious mind affects those parts of the body that are related to the present lifetime issues, with past life pains and patterns. For example, problems with the eyes and vision and optic nerves, suggests that the person does not want to see something. This happens to a lot of children who have been abused. They do not want to see that

96

that abuse happened and so they can't see. (They develop poor eyesight -- usually needing glasses.) The past life involved would be one in which the person stopped others from seeing or one in which the person himself was stopped from seeing.

Back pains are very interesting indeed. Doctors cannot guarantee relief from back pains. People go to chiropractors. Sometimes they get relief, most of the time temporary, if at all. Well, what does the back do? It supports the entire frame of the body. It is responsible for the activity of the body. And that is what back pains and problems are all about - responsibility! Clear up the mental and emotional issues surrounding their ability (or inability) to be responsible, and the back pain will disappear!

Show me someone who has back problems and I will show you someone who needs to be responsible for some part of his life and is not doing so. In some cases, I have had clients with severe back pains that were totally responsible for everyone else. But guess what? They were still not being responsible for themselves and their own present life issues. Thus the back pain.

Below is a list of areas of the body and the issues that they represent. This list is by no means complete but I am adding to it each and every day as my work and research warrants.

I have discovered for instance that most people with very poor eyesight, the type that wear old coke bottle thick glasses, usually did a hostile act against another in a past life. What is a hostile act? It is an act of violence, force or subterfuge used to make others wrong or weak or defenseless. The reason for the poor eyesight is that the unconscious mind does not want to see what it did in the past. This is only one example of how past lives influence the body and bodily organs. In your work, I know you will discover many more correlations between past lives and present time illnesses and difficulties.

Reviewing the lifetimes where you (or your client) hurt others in the exact same body parts as to where you suffer will usually cause the pain to reduce and even disappear. Of course, you should also run all original incidents where you were hurt in those body parts by others.

| Problem Areas | Problems |
| --- | --- |
| Head | Leadership Problems |
| Ears | Don't want to hear something |
| Eyes | Don't want to see something |
| Throat (Teeth, gums) | Not communicating |
| Back | Not being responsible |
| Legs | Difficulties supporting self/others |
| Stomach | Problem with security and safety |
| Sexual Organs | Problem surviving |
| Heart | Difficulties with love |

# C h a p t e r 10

## Personal Power with PLT

We live in an age where it seems that many people have little self-respect or self-esteem. Consultants to the state of California agreed that this was the number one problem to confront all people, especially young Americans. If a person does not possess self-respect, how can he ever have respect for others? You see, in this universe, you can only get what you create. If you create a life that is fun and exciting then you life is fun and exciting. If you create a life that is boring and tiring, then that too is what you create. Self-esteem and personal power also have to be created as well.

Whatever you want out of life, you can only get it by having already clearly created it within your awareness and mind. By doing this, you tell your neuro-circuits of your mind and body to turn on to that reality that you created. Once those neuro-circuits (circuits of awareness) turn on, you then preceive that reality. If you think this too deep or heady, it works like this. A young boy decides that he wants to be a research scientist when he grows up. Twenty years later, the young man is now a research scientist living and breathing the issues of his environment. Here we see that the young boy kept the image of what he wanted in his mind and then created that reality.

In the USA, I have noticed many people have no sense of personal power. For the people that seem to possess personal power, it is usually ego power -- the "I've got everything under control" mentality -- or false power. The illusion of power is false power. There are many people who are actually powerless but act as if they are powerful. But real power is true personal power. It requires personal power, energy and skill to cause changes within your life and being.

Could you use more power in your life? Maybe in business? Relationships?

The fact is that most people in the world need more power in themselves. Once they can establish that personal power, they can then then have power in their world and life. Power is the most feared thing in this world. Many people are afraid of power because power requires responsibility and control. This is why they prefer to work a regular job rather than own their own business. Imagine how your life would be different if you had power in your life.

## _HOW TO ACCESS YOUR PERSONAL POWER_

As you look back into your past lives, you will discover lifetimes in which you displayed incredible strength and courage and personal power. The theory to develop personal power instantaneously is: get back to those lifetimes of power, strength and courage and you can reawaken those realities now. Once these abilities are brought into the now, you can use them.

Here is how it is done. The following transcript is a basic interaction between myself and a client who wanted to access more personal power and control in himself and his life.

R: You would like to get more power in yourself and your life?

Bill: Yes. There are things that I don't do with my life that I would do if I simply had more power, personal power!

R: Can you imagine your special movie screen where you play the tapes of how you are now in your selected environment and the way that you would act if you had more personal power.

Bill: Okay. The environment is work. I need more personal power to get people at the office to listen to me and my ideas.

R: All right. Look at the movie screen and see yourself oozing personal power. When you can do that nod your head! (Bill nods) How do you handle the office environment now that you have more personal power?

Bill: I deal with things more authoratively. I have a strong presence. People respond to me.

R: Is this the kind of personal power that you would like to have?

Bill: Yes. That's it!

R: Okay, Bill. I want you to notice the kind of power that you need and want. With that I want you to travel 500 feet up into the air and tell me when you are there! Bill nods his head. All right, I want you to start to descend towards the earth. As you descend, you will go into the past life that contains all those power and abilities that you require to have the personal power you now desire! Once you have landed, I want you to tell me. (Bill nods). Bill, I want you to watch the past life personal self that you were during times of interaction or negotiation with others. Did you have personal power then?

Bill: Yes. I had charisma. The way that I held myself and the like.

R: Watch the way that you held your body then. Now make those same changes in your present life body. Notice the way that you breathed back then. Match the breathing. Notice how you held your eyes. Match that. Notice how you spoke..loud, soft, firm, short sentences, long ones? Match all that now. Now finally put yourself inside of him and noticed how he felt when he was with others. Feel all those feelings.

Bill, you have now cloned most of that past personality in regards to personal power. What I want you to do next is to locate any other missing factors that might be important to having personal power. Anything that is missing and that you should have you can now clone and add to your present personality build. Tell me when you have done all of this!

Bill: Okay.

R: How do you feel?

Bill: Powerful. It's like an energy flowing through my entire body. It's like sparks. Wow.

R: Think of those areas of your life now where you want to have that personal power and energy. How does it seem to you now?

Bill: Well now when I think of having to get things done, I know that I have the power to cause that change. I will be very interested to see how this changes things at work.

R: Think of something now that you have put off doing in your life because you did not have a large amount of personal power or energy.

Bill: Okay! It seems ridiculous to have stopped myself because I did not think I had enough power to do that.

## COMMENTS:

Power has several definitions:

1. The ability to create, maintain and destroy your position or attitude in space.

2. The ability to do work and get things done.

3. The ability to have fast and accurate perceptions and minimal reaction times.

4. The ability to confront anything that you desire to handle.

Of course, there are many more definitions for power but the ones above fit the bill. If you find that you are lacking in any of the four definitions above, then you might want to work on turning on and amplifying your personal power. The lack of personal power is what holds any person back from doing and achieving the things they desire.

The subject of Power is dealt with thoroughly in **THE MAGICK OF POWER** book by Richard A. Greene and the Audio and Video cassettes of the same name. These can be ordered through **Next Step Publications, P.O. Box 1403, Nashua, NH 03061 (800) 326-0369**. Call for prices and orders.

# Chapter 11

## Healing with PLT

Let's talk about using PLT as a tool or technique for healing. As you learned earlier, the mind is the source of all illnesses or problems. Like a computer program, the mind does what it is programmed to do. Illnesses and problems are computer mind programs as well. PLT is the process and technique to change and alter the mental programs of the mind.

The first important requirement for PLT to be successful is that you (if you are working on yourself) or your client be willing and able to confront the problem, illness or situation. When the client is ready to confront his problem or illness, he is well on the way to healing. This is because once the problem or illness is confronted, it is only a matter of reviewing the incident in order to clear and reach a "release." If one is not willing to confront the illness, problem or past life, then one cannot handle the problem and achieve the desired results.

## AXIOMS OF PAST LIFE THERAPY

o *NO ILLNESS IN THE BODY CAN OCCUR UNLESS IT HAS BEEN CREATED IN THE MIND*

o *ANY ILLNESS IN THE MIND WILL EVENTUALLY MANIFEST IN THE BODY*

o *RELEASE THE PAST LIFE BY VIEWING IT AND THE ILLNESS WILL RELEASE FROM THE MIND AND IMMEDIATELY OR EVENTUALLY FROM THE BODY*

o *EVERY ILLNESS HAS A PAST LIFE CONNECTION*

## PAIN CONTROL AND RELIEF

Past life therapy is one of the most excellent tools for rapid pain relief and reduction. Essentially, the process is to feel or recall the pain, locate what part of the body that pain resides in. By doing that, you are now ready to return to that life time that contains the incident that caused that pain, in that part of the body.

## PLT & BACK PAIN

Here is a script of a session with a client who had trmendous lower back pains. He would become so incapacitated that the only relief he had was to lie in tub of hot water for hours at a time. He tried chiropractors but there was no relief and he did not want to take drugs to relieve the pain.

R: What can I do for you today?

Cl: I have had terrific back problems for several weeks now. I have been to doctors and chiropractors and none of them have done much good for getting rid of the pain.

R: Do you have any problems with past life therapy?

Cl: I don't even know what it is. If it can get rid of my pain, I don't care what it is!

R: All right then. Just follow my directions and let's see what happens. OK?

Cl: Sure.

R: Recall the back pain that you have been suffering. Notice the type of pain and where it is located in your body.

Cl: Smiles. That's easy. I feel the pain right now. It's acute and in my lower back. In the center of my lower back.

R: Good. Now remember that feeling of pain and its location as you float up in the air about 500 feet. Tell me when you can be up in the air. (He nods) All right. Start to descend towards the earth but when you land you will be back in the life time that is the cause for your present life back problems.

Cl: I've landed.

R: Tell me. What do you see?

Cl: I can't see anything. It's dark. I only see blackness.

R: Is there anything else?

Cl: Not that I can see.

R: All right. Turn the darkness to light. Sort of like turning night into daytime. When you do that, you will be able to see images and pictures.

Cl: I'm turning it light. Oh yeah. I see people dressed like Romans. Its dark - nighttime.

R: All right, what happens next?

106

Cl: I am there because it is a late night meeting. A secret meeting.

R: Continue.

Cl: I am talking to three men seated at a table in front of me. I know the one in the middle real well. We are talking, he's angry but he keeps a smile on his face. He rises up from the table, walks towards me. He comes up beside me puts his arm around me. I stand there. He takes his hand from around me. He keeps talking then suddenly I feel an intense pain.

R: Where do you feel the pain?

Cl: In my back.

R: At the same place where it hurts in the present life?

Cl: Yes. Exactly.

R: What happened in that life time to cause the pain?

Cl: He stabbed me in the back with a knife.

R: What happens next.

Cl: He's still smiling. He watches me falling to the ground. He then kneels in front of me so I can see his face. Then he turns the knife and keeps turning it.

R: What happens next.

Cl: My body dies.

R: What causes the death of the body?

Cl: The way that he stabbed me. It was with such force it went right through my spinal column and severed my spinal cord.

R: Does this incident have an earlier beginning? Is there something about this incident that you have not seen but need to?

Cl: Yeah. There's something earlier.

R: All right then, move to the earlier beginning of the incident and run that.

Cl: That guy and I grew up together. Out fathers knew each other. We were good friends when growing up. I wanted to help people and he simply wanted power and control. He did many things that I was disturbed about. Because I would not join him, he and I grew apart. As we became older and powerful, I was going to have a position of power greater than his. He knew that if I had that power, I might make decisions and create legislations that would hinder his desire and greed. He arranged to have me meet late at night with him and some others. Supposedly when we met, they were going to aid me. I believed him because I did not think he would ever be so greedy or vicious as to murder me.

R: Now, run the rest of the incident. Pay particular attention to when the knife goes into your body and the pain.

Cl: Okay.

R: Is there anything about that incident that keeps it in place or is the incident releasing?

Cl: The incident is releasing.

R: How does your back feel to you now?

Cl: (He moves around a little.) There's a little bit of pain left but much of it is gone.

R: Now. The final piece. Is there anything that happened in your present life that  resembles or parallels that past life time?

Cl: (He thinks about it.) Yes. I was working with a man who suddenly changed his mind and turned on me. We were going to do some things together, it looked good. Then he changed.

R: How did you feel about that now?

Cl: Wow. I feel like I was stabbed in the back. He turned on me and stabbed me in the back. When that happened in this lifetime, is when my back pain started. Wow. I never thought that my back pain and that person's actions were connected.

R: I see that you look different. Your face looks relaxed. How does the pain seem to you now?

Cl: It's gone. Completely gone.

R: Let's test it. Is there anything that you couldn't do when you had the back pain?

Cl: Sure. I couldn't bend over and touch my toes.

R: Let's try that. Slowly now, bend over and touch your toes.

Cl: He bends right over and touches his toes.

R: Well you didn't wait too long to do that. How do you feel?

Cl: Great. The pain is gone.

## *PLT & ENDOMYETRIOSIS*

Just to be sure that you get this process and technique down, here is another past life experience with a woman who used to get endomyetriosis. Her complaint was that she suffered terrific pain in her stomach region. She had been to several doctors who told her the only ways to deal with this endomyetriosis would be surgery or to have a baby. The latter solution, having a baby, might work they added, but it was a 50-50 chance.

This woman was a very active person, and because of the endomyetriosis, she had to tone it down since the pain was so great.

R: You have discussed your problem with me. Can you get the pain and discomfort associated with your endomyetriosis?

Cl: Yes.

R: Okay, go 500 feet up into the air and tell me when you are there.

Cl: I'm there.

R: Now, start to descend towards the earth. When you touch down, I want you to be back in the primary lifetime that is the cause for your present time problem and pains associated with the endomyetriosis.

Cl: I've landed.

R: Describe the scenery and background to me.

Cl: It's like back in the early days of England. There's a castle.

R: What type of body do you have?

Cl: I am a female. A girl.

R: About how old are you at this time?

Cl: I am about 15 years old. (She starts to cry)

R: What's happening?

Cl: They are taking it away.

R: Taking what away?

Cl: They are taking my baby away.

R: Your baby?

Cl: Yes. I just gave birth. This woman comes in. She is my mother and she is telling me they must get rid of the baby. She (my mother) tells me I must get rid of my baby.

R: And how must you get rid of your baby?

Cl: I must kill it.

R: Why?

Cl: I don't know why. (Crying) She tells me it is no good and that I must destroy it.

R: What happens next?

Cl: I destroy the baby.

R: How do you destroy the baby?

Cl: I drown it. My mother is watching me.

R: All right. Run that incident several times, tell me when you are finished.

Cl: I have seen it. (She is still crying.)

R: Is there something more to this incident that you have not seen.

Cl: I have not seen who the father is.

R: Take a look, by moving to an earlier time in the incident.

Cl: Ohh! It's my father. My father is the king in the castle. It's his baby. My mother knows this and that's why I have to destroy it.

R: All right, run that a few times. Does the incident release?

Cl: Not yet!

R: Go to that part of the incident that stops the incident from releasing.

Cl: My father comes to my room. We are alone. He takes me sexually.

R: Does he rape you? Take you by force?

Cl: I don't know.

R: Move to that part that stops the incident from clearing and see it with clarity.

Cl: Ohhh. (A sudden release is indicated by the relaxation of her face muscles) I *seduced* him! I led him on to do that to me.

R: How does the incident seem to you now?

Cl: Released.

R: How do you feel now?

Cl: I don't feel any pain right now, but I will be better able to tell later when I try to exercise.

R: Okay, but take it easy and please get back to me.


She called the next morning apologizing for not calling me the night before. She told me that she did about 40 minutes of trampoline exercise and that there was no pain whatsoever. She said that she kept expecting the pain to come back but it did not. She added that normally trying to do trampoline exercises (which require a lot of jumping and bouncing) would hurt so much that she couldn't do them. But now, she was looking forward to her daily workout on the trampoline.

### *NOTES*

Remember that when you try to use this material for yourself, you might have difficulty at first. Especially if you are in pain yourself. In that case, you could instruct someone to aid you. Tell them the questions you want them to ask you.

If you do not have someone to help, you could always ask your questions on a cassette recorder and play the questions back to you one at a time until you get to the lifetime, the incident and the release from the pain and conflict induced by that past life experience.

When you work past life therapy to relieve pain or discomfort, make sure that you work the incident so that it releases completely.

Usually, if the pain or discomfort continues, that is a sure sign that the incident has not been released.

If the incident releases and the pain and discomfort continues, then move to an earlier lifetime and run that incident in that lifetime.

At worst, there should be a reduction of pain. At best, total relief.

---

# Chapter 12

## The Patterns of Past Lives

When you run past lives, you will discover that there is pattern - a similarity or correspondence between the present life pattern and the past life pattern. Typically, you notice that it seems like you are running the same pattern again and again.

When I was asked to teach a seminar to some students at Boston College, I remember that there was one student who came to me. He ran out a past life in which he was an athlete runner. One day as he ran, he tripped over a rock, broke his legs. He gave up the athletics for a more cerebral profession in this case law and philosophy.

He was totally amazed as he did not know what he would see in that past life, but it reflected the present life accurately. He told me that he had been an excellent skier and that he had wanted to ski in the Olympics. But one day while skiing, he tripped and broke his legs. He could walk now but couldn't ski like he needed and wanted to. And, he was studying law, and would soon be taking the bar exams.

Many times, there is a pattern of moving from one type or pattern to its opposite. For example, the torturer of a medeval kingdom, is now the healer. The problem with this opposition is that there are still the basic elements within the personality that revert back to those past life times. This is why we hear about surgeons who do brutal surgery or unwanted or unneeded surgery. The torturer is still in the mind, even though the present life profession is to be a surgeon.

This pattern is especially clear when we pay attention to police officers and criminals. The police officer has to become a criminal (think and act like one) in order to capture one. In some cases, the police officer is a criminal with a badge.

But what got the person into law enforcement in the first place? Research into past lives indicates that the person may have first been a legal oriented person i.e., a lawyer, or a judge or a senator. Perhaps one who legislates laws. Then in a later lifetime, the person becomes a law enforcement agent.

One interesting point that is proven over and over again in past life work, is that any person who has a fixation or obsession about one thing, actually is trying to fight the inclination and internal drive to be the opposite. Here are some examples:

People who are so obsessed about prevention of child abuse, are really fighting the internal desire to be a child abuser.

People who are so obsessed about morality, are fighting internal urges to be immoral.

People who are so obsessed about fighting pornography, are

fighting internal pornographic urges.

Now please be sure to understand what I am saying. I am not saying that anyone involved in fighting an issue is actually the opposite. I am saying if there is an obsession about fighting an issue, it usually becomes personal, and in that case, the person is actually fighting their own urges.

These are the patterns of past lives.

You might ask, well Rich, if this is true, then how should one be towards any issue?

I would say, to be concerned, involved, but detached. No thing should become so personal that it is a matter of control. Here is an example:

A reformed drunk is obnoxious and intolerant of others drinking alcohol. This in itself shows that the person has not really dealt with the drinking at all. The same goes for smoking or anything else.

Born again Christians, intolerant of any other religion but their own, is also an example of this past life pattern. Why do they need to convert anyone else? Because they don't really believe that they believe. Change everyone else, make them believe what you avow you believe and it becomes easy to believe it yourself.

## *PREDICTING RELATIONSHIPS*

Wouldn't it be nice, if you were starting a relationship, to know how you and your partner interact with each other? Wouldn't that information save you a lot of money, time and hassle? Many smart people go to astrologers and psychics for such information. But past life recall offers a tremendous possibility to know the outcome of a relationship or the personality of the person you are involved with **before** you get too involved. This past life information would have saved many divorces, bad marriages, and destructive relationships.

Why does past life recall predict present and future relationships? Because the past determines how we handle the present and the future. For instance, a person who is used to handling problems by becoming angry, will probably continue to be that way until some better and more appropriate behavior appears.

## The Past Life Connection

I will now share with you an example of a past life connection and how it influences the present lifetime. For the example, I will use the experience of a client I worked with.

When he was about five years old in the present life, he remembered seeing in his mind's eye, a bald headed man, with piercing eyes, wearing a black robe, making gestures in the air with his hands and lightning-like energy coming from his hands. For some reason, in some intuitive way, he knew that he was that person.

At about this same time, he experienced states of consciousness that he later discovered were known as Samahdi - ultimate states of awareness in which one becomes united with the universal, cosmic consciousness.

When he could first read, he studied and read about mythologies of the Greeks and Romans. Astrology was one of my first intuitive knowings. He knew that the planets and the stars exerted some sort of influence on the affairs of humanity.

He discovered that he had psychic powers and especially an

ability to heal with a simple touch that is powerful and evident, especially today.

At the age of 14, he was proficient in Karate and music. He played guitar and wrote songs. One day, while in Boston, he entered a book store on Tremont St. called Booklane (now defunct). While he was in the store there was a book for sale at half-price called, "Magick In Theory and Practice" by Aleister Crowley. Interestingly enough, the name of the Author, not the title of the book literally jumped into his mind. He knew he had to own this book. He bought the book, but to his dismay, did not understand anything in it. He lent it to a friend of a friend — who was a self-proclaimed witch. About a year later, the book was returned to him, but now when he read it, he seemed to know it inside and out.

When he was about 18 years old, he managed an occult book store in Cambridge, Massachusetts known as the Aquarian Age. Many psychics and astrologers and just curious people came to the store. One woman who was a truly gifted psychic, told him how she saw him in his very last lifetime. She said, "You were an old man. You looked Chinese, but you weren't. And you were smoking a pipe!"

Another regular visitor to the store, was a man named Jimmy Omar. He came to find the spiritually awakened people knowing that such people would come to a bookstore like the Aquarian Age. One night, he and Jimmy was there when a man happened to wander in. Jimmy started talking about consciousness and the master-level consciousness to this wanderer. He was partly paying attention, when he suddenly heard Jimmy say to that man, "You are a master, with a Buddha consciousness. Just like that guy over there!"

Well, he was the only other guy in the store. He listened on. Jimmy said, "There are markings that the body possesses." That was it. He came out from behind the counter and asked Jimmy about it. Imagine! All this time Jimmy was coming to the store and only now did he tell him about this masterhood stuff. Jimmy mentioned that he had a five-pointed star on his forehead. He quickly went to the toilet where there was a mirror. He looked at his reflection and saw a five-pointed star etched in blue in the mirror. (The pentagram or five-pointed star indicates a spiritually evolved being who has come back to the Earth plane to be a healer and teacher.)

About a week later, Aleister Crowley's autobiography came out. The book contained pictures of Crowley. Suddenly, the name that jumped out at him when he was 14 years old, plus the image that he had seen for so long, that he knew that he had been in a previous incarnation, were all there. So too was the picture of Crowley later in life, where he (Crowley) looked Chinese, but he was not (Crowley was English) smoking a pipe.

The psychic Peggy came in a day or so after Crowley's autobiography arrived. She looked through it. He watched her as she did so. She looked up at me and smiled and said, "Do you know who you were now?"

He smiled and shook his head in the affirmative.

He had been developing his magickal and psychic and astrological skills beyond where they were naturally. At about 19 to 20 years old, he was on a famous Boston talk radio show - WBZ Larry Glick show. Glick had a late night show that was quite popular. Larry is into hypnosis, which led to all kinds of topics about the occult, ESP and the like.

He was Larry's guest one night for about three hours where he covered all kinds of topics about spiritual and psychic matters. As you might imagine, the phone rang off the hook at the studio.

The most interesting situation to emerge out of that radio show was an invitation to a dinner party thrown by James and Adele Fahey. For those of you not in the know, James is the author of the Pacific War Diaries - a very popular book.

At the dinner party, he met Steve Leonard and Marian. Marian it turns out was a practicing psychic. As they sat at the table, he felt on a psychic level how he knew several of the people there. He looked at Steve and told him, "Steve, You and I were brothers in Atlantis and oh-by the way, I was Aleister Crowley." Steve looked at him with that vacant stare of disbelief bordering on the "he-must be-insane" stare.

Steve, it turns out was good friends with a man named Bill Swygard. Bill was known around parts of the country for his awareness techniques - some of which deal with past life recall and memory.

During a phone conversation with Steve, he was told the following:

Bill Swygard had come into Steve's bookstore. There were Crowley books as well as other magick oriented books in stock. Swygard picked up the books by Crowley and then said to Steve, "You and this guy Crowley were brothers in Atlantis."

Steve asked Swygard if Crowley could have incarnated by now. (Crowley died in 1947 - he was born in 1952). Swygard answered, "I don't think so! But let's check it out."

Bill was married to Diane (who he never met) but apparently she would go into trance and check things out. In this case, she went into trance and said that Crowley was indeed back in the body and that he did not live to far from here. ("Here" was Massachusetts. He was living in Brighton-Allston, Massachusetts then.)

At this point Steve asked, "What about the name _____?" Diane in trance replied, "That's him!"

Now even though he had all these experiences, he was still a skeptic. After all, he knew that there were at least 665 others in the USA alone that believed they were Crowley. One guy in California, shaved his head, something Crowley would do, wrote atrocius poetry (something Crowley didn't do) and declared he was Crowley incarnated because he looked like him. (But with a shaved head, anyone could look like Crowley. Even Telly Savalas could play Crowley!)

The only problem is that Crowley on a return visit to Earth would not repeat what he did earlier. (He have even heard recently that there is a gentleman, living not far from him who is a successful, practicing lawyer who claims to be Crowley as well. It is doubtful that Crowley would come back as a lawyer - Crowley had only contempt for such a profession.)

Alice Bailey, a woman who trance channeled a Tibetan muckee-muck (long before trance channeling was in) stated in one book that if you were to live a life of spiritual development, you would incarnate in the opposite sign. Whether this is true or not still remains to be researched - BUT Crowley was a Libra - while he is an Aries - the opposite sign. In addition, Crowley had Leo rising at four degrees, while he has Aquarius rising 3-4 degrees — again the opposite sign.

One day, while doing a magickal work of getting in touch with his Holy Guardian Angel (HGA for short) something that all true occultists must do at one time or another in whatever fashion they may, his guardian angel appeared. THe HGA called itself AIWASS. This was the name of Crowley's HGA. Now he wasn't overly impressed by this since he had read some of Crowley's works and therefore already knew his HGA's name.

Ever skeptical, but never one to waste a good moment, he thought something like, "Aiwass, now that you are here, how about some real evidence that I was Crowley." Of course, he expected Aiwass to vanish. Instead, Aiwass says, "Sure." (What trick does Aiwass have up his sleeve? he wondered.)

Aiwass says to him, "Spell out your name and work it out numerically!" (When he says that Aiwass speaks, he means that it was like a voice in his head.) He did so and got the number 683. He was at a total loss. "Aiwass", he said, "If this is supposed to be significant, you got me." Suddenly, the voice in his head said, "No, do it this way!" Aiwass showed him another way in which his name was spelt. This time the number he got was "666" which was much more significant since this was an important number to Crowley that Crowley obtained out of the book of revelations.

He also remembered an even earlier past life where he was a disciple John of Jesus Christ and the supposed author of the Book of Revelations. This made incredible sense in that John followed the teachings of Jesus (which were quite magickal regardless of what the Born-agains might claim), wrote the Book of Revelations (which was actually an introduction to the Qabalistic/Magickal teachings of that time and has been totally mistranslated - just as the whole Bible has).

As Crowley, perhaps the one book that most influenced him was the Book of Revelations. No wonder - he Crowley) wrote it during the incarnation as John.

Most importantly, in understanding and learning about his Crowley incarnation, he learned a lot about himself and why he did what he did. Below are just some of the relationships between the two:

## Crowley

_• Inherited a large amount of money. And squandered it. No business sense. Died poor.

• Used drugs to alter consciousness. Became a heroin addict including needles/syringes.

• Sensitivity and imagination that isolated him from others yet led him to the study of Magick.

• Had a sardonic wit and humor.

• Very sexual - even acted as head of a sex magick group.

• Developed new modes and styles of magick.

• Had difficulties with relationships and marriage.

• Attained high levels of consciousness and awareness. Applied scientific methods to consciousness.

• Crowley was an Aesthetic - poet, writer, entertainer, teacher.

## Him

• Born poor. Had to learn to be a businessman. Hates waste of money and resources and talents.

• Very sexual.

•Sardonic wit and humor.

• Difficulties with relationships and marriage but is changing those difficulties by working on himself.

• Attained high levels of consciousness and awareness. Present life has been employed as an engineer and consultant. Applied those standards to Magick.

• Developed a new level of Bio-Magick.

• Experimented with drugs and their effects on consciousness. Aversion to hard drugs (all drugs as of this writing) especially those requiring needles/syringes.

•Writer, communicator, teacher/trainer, entertainer.


### Author's Comments

There is so much more that cannot be put into this account. But it was obvious that where Crowley left off, he began. Outside of the magick and high levels of awareness, he has striven to divest himself of Crowley - as that persona has truly been more of a hindrance than an asset.

It is my experience that most of the people who claim to have been Crowley, are looking for power, admiration, and all the other traits that would raise one up from insignificance and low self-confidence. But regardless of who you were in the past, you must earn your wings so to speak and not rely on past laurels.

It is of no usefulness to him or to anyone to blindly believe that the personality known as _____ was once a personality known as Aleister Crowley. After all, the excesses and abuses that

Crowley displayed, he has had to rectify in this life.

Several people who have questioned this past life connection have expected him to have specific details of the Crowley incarnation. This does not usually happen. Oh yes, there may be some periods of intense detail, but not necessarily of the entire incarnation. After all, he is here on Earth to live this life and use his skills and assets in a resourceful way.

Truly the only good that comes from any recognition of any past incarnation, is simply to know where you have come from and therefore know what troubles and problems will most likely plague you so that you can change them. In addition, the assets and viable skills can also be known and developed further in the present incarnation as well.

By the bye, my research of A.C. is that he was not an evil man - Crowley was an egotist that made him (A.C.) a loner and caused him isolation in his life. He on the other hand, in this present lifetime has experienced and lived with that isolation and is now working on removing that from his life.

Whenever you run a past life, look at the difficulties that confronted you in that incarnation. Those same difficulties will be with you now in this life. They may seem to be different — yet they are the same. For instance, addiction to drugs one lifetime - addiction to food, sex, chocolates, another person or what have you in this one. The pattern of addiction is still there, but not necessarily to the same item.

He hope this helps you in your work.

# Chapter 13

## Handling Difficulties

This chapter covers the most likely difficulties that will occur during your practice of Past Life Therapy on yourself or with others. Included in this chapter are techniques that I have developed to handle those specific problems and difficulties.

### *PLT PROBLEM #1 - Difficulty Entering a Past Life*

The most usual problem that you may face with PLT is that you or your client wont go into a past life. If you use the 500 feet method to enter into a past life, you may not enter into one because there isn't one. No lifetime -- no place to descend into. If this should be the case, be sure to check that the original incident doesn't begin in early present life. A check of the early present life should present the original incident that causes the present life problem.

126

If there is a past lifetime that contains the original incident and you do not land in it, it might also be that the incident is so traumatic that your unconscious mind tries to protect you from remembering the past life incident. In this case, you only need to do the following steps:

1. Relax more. You can do this by practicing some hypnotic work - techniques are contained in the appendix.

2. Just let whatever images come to mind. Don't edit.

3. Look at the lifetime just a little at time. Don't try to see it all at once.

### *PROBLEM #2 - All There is  is Darkness*

You land into a past life but everything is dark and you can't see anything.

Whenever the past life incident is dark it means that there was trauma or unconsciousness or death of some sort. In this case,  either you can back up the lifetime incident to when there was light, (this will probably bring you back to before there was unconsciousness or death or trauma.) Once back to when the incident turns to light, run the incident again from beginning to end as you have learned earlier.

A second way that you can handle a "dark incident" is to "step outside" of the incident as if you were looking at frames in a film. As you step outside of the film, turn the dark frames (which are the traumatic incident) to white. As the frames become lighter, you will find that you can see the content inside the frames. In other words, the past original incident becomes clearer and is now available to the consdious mind awareness.

127

Once the frames are clear and lightened, step back into the incident and run it from beginning to end as many times as it takes to release the original incident.

### *PROBLEM #3 - Stuck Pictures*

You get stuck in an incident. That is, as you run the incident you come to a situation where you can't move the pictures forward or back, they are just stuck plain and simple.

In this incident, you experienced some emotion that made you stuck. For instance, "frozen with fear." In this case, find the particular feeling or emotion that you experienced in the original incident. Then, re-experience the emotion(s) or feeling - actually try to copy the exact feeling or emotion. (By duplicating the feeling or emotion, you release it.) Now the past life incident should now become unstuck and be able to move.

### *PROBLEM #4 - Seeing Several Different Lifetimes*

You go back into the past life and suddenly, you see several different lifetimes simultaneously.

In this case, locate the earliest lifetime of all the lifetimes that you see. Remember, you always seek to find the earliest lifetime and so you do the same here.

By the way, the reason why the lifetimes all group together is because all the lifetimes have a common element or thread. For instance, if you are running a lifetime in the 1700's when you were stabbed in the stomach and suddenly see lifetimes in medieval England and another in Ancient Egypt, you will find that the theme of being stabbed in the stomach is consistent in each of the lifetimes that are grouped together.


## PROBLEM #5 - Problem Doesn't Release

You run the lifetime original incident but it doesn't release. Check your part in that lifetime. For instance, you might see yourself at first being the person who is "being done to." If the incident doesn't release, run the original lifetime incident as the one who is "doing to." For example, if you run a lifetime trying to resolve stomach problems, and you recall being stabbed in the stomach, but your present stomach problems continue, run the lifetime again, but from the point of view of the person who did the stabbing.

A woman I worked with in Washington, D.C. came to me with throat problems. She felt that the root of her problem was emotional. She went back into an earlier lifetime where she remembered being a little girl who had been sexually assaulted by two older men. After they finished, the men were going to let her go, but she turned and said to the men, "I know who you are! I'm telling my father. He's powerful. He'll get you for this!" The men looked at each other. Then one of the men grab her and quickly cuts her throat. At this point, the incident should have had some sort of release, but it didn't. I had her review the incident several times but nothing seemed to happen.

Suddenly, she had a release. She said, "Oh my God, I wasn't the little girl, I was the man who cut her throat!" With that, the incident cleared up and released and she let go of it. Her throat problems cleared up quickly and immediately.

### *PROBLEM #6 - You Get Sleepy /Tired Running the Past Life*

You try to run the incident but each time you get tired and cannot go any further with it.

Most likely in this incident you will come across hypnosis, poison/drugs, or a specialized case called Energy Implants. These energy implants happened very early in the history of this planet and on other planets. It is the way in which a technological planetary government keeps its citizens under control.

Implants were quick. They took less than 10 seconds in many cases, and contained all kinds of commands and influences to stop a person from indulging in certain behaviors.

The way to check for an implant is to simply ask, "Is there an energy force being used on you?" or "Are you using an energy force on somebody?"

Then run the incident several times.

### *PROBLEM #7 - The Lifetime Incident Doesn't End*

The incident runs on and on and doesn't seem to have an end.

Usually this is an example of an implant. It creates a never resolving incident that just runs on and on. Run the implant as in Problem #6.

# Chapter 14

## Changing the Future
## by Reliving the Past

The following material indicates why people hold onto the past, how they do it and how by holding onto the past, people actually influence their present and future.

Have you ever met a person that was basically depressed and down? Even if he lifted himself up and was happy for a time, simply revert back into the depression? How does a person do this to himself?

Here is the basic method:

The person has had some sort of past experience and has made either a visual (such as a mental picture) or an audio representation (such as a voice or a certain noise) that was present when the incident took place. Somewhere in the present life, he comes across the representation either in audio mode and/or visual mode that then turns on the depression. The pictures do not have to be an actual representation of a memory or expreience. Any picture could suffice.

For example, why do some people cry when they see a picture or drawing of a religious personality such as Jesus Christ? Some picture is running through their heads and yet we know it is not a present life memory since we can safely assume that Jesus was not around in the present life.

But whatever might be an abstract picture from the present life point of perspective (such as Jesus Christ on the cross) may actually be a real memory impression when reviewed from the perspective of past lives.

Many time in your own experience or those of your clients if you do this work professionally, you will find that you get a strange picture or image in your mind. From this present life point of view there may be nothing - no association to explain the strange picture or image of the mind. And yet, many times when a person embarks on the past life adventure, he will come upon a past life where suddenly he sees that image or picture and it makes sense. He suddenly realizes that the picture in his mind was related to another lifetime.

The reason for the intrusion of past life images or pictures onto the present life consciousness is because each life time that is buried in your awareness actually influences your past lives. They are influencing your abilities, attitudes, and fears, even now. In fact, they influence the very way you do life. Oh, by the way - your past lives don't just influence your life, it actually creates it.

Every attitude, belief, fear etc. that you have, comes from

somewhere. The law of Cause and Effect takes place here. So, all you have to do is to return to the source from whence the original fear, belief, etc, originated, and release that particular attitude, fear or belief.

It has been shown many times in this work, that a person's present life comes from the past life. (This is not to say that future lives are not influencing the present life as well!)

So a person has a fear of snakes or escalators, elevators, heights, closeness, etc. These fears and phobias obviously affect the client's present life. By eradicating those fears and the like, you change the quality and performance of the person's life; thus proving that the past affects the future.

Another thing that you must be aware of is that the past life forms specific patterns. For instance, the emotional pattern known as hate is a counter-pattern (or counter-emotion) to the emotional pattern of love. The emotion of hate can only manifest when there is first a pattern of love.

In understanding this you discover that a person can never hate something or someone unless there was first a decision to love. The pattern of hate is as follows:

1) Decide that you love something or someone.

2) Have that something or someone miscommunicate so that you feel or experience betrayal, death, pain, or loss.

3) You will now have a good dose of hatred.

Unresolved love affairs that turn to hatred are still happening out of the original agreement -- love.

Here is another example of past life patterns.

A criminal in the present life. How did he get here?

1) First, there may have been a love of justice or law -- he becomes a judge or lawyer. He is so severe in his meting out of justice; that the law is for all and no one stands above it. He causes a thief to have his hands cut off for stealing.

2) Now comes another lifetime in law enforcement. Here there is no difference between the criminal and the law enforcement person. After all, they must both think alike. The law enforcement agent is the criminal with the badge.

3) The next life time, having already established the person as being a criminal in mind and thoughts (as the law enforcement agent), he now becomes the criminal.

Now this is a sketch of how one shifts from one extreme to another from a past life to present life.

In this world, we are encouraged to seek a righteous path of belief and action. In doing so, there is a tendency to become narrow-minded -- thinking in terms of rightness and wrongness. "I am right." "You are wrong."

Whenever a person comes from this base of thinking, he is setting up to go into an opposing lifetime. Why would a person be so righteous? Because he is afraid, insecure and unconfident. Being righteous helps them to bolster themselves up. This is most evident among the born again Christians who think they are right, they have the only weay and everyone who does not think and act like them is wrong and damned.

No one is ever right or wrong!

No learning is ever right or wrong!

Instead there is only power, elegance creativity and spirit!

All people come from what they know best. A person in the ghetto can't think in terms of millions of dollars achieved through international business. It does not mean that such a person can't imagine this someday. It simply means that such a person is not presently exposed to that kind of reality. Consequently his selected options of how to make money coincide with the reality of what his background environment allows.

Intolerance comes from the fact that people are insecure and afraid of others. So to be safe, it is only necessary, to make others exactly like yourself. This is the basic of intolerance.

When you work with past life therapy, the basis of each emotion or human strength and weakness, becomes evident. Not only will you learn why such things happen but also how they happen. This is information that is important and powerful not just for yourself and your clients (should you do this work professionally) but for the entire human race as well.

# Chapter 15

## Other Possibilities of PLT

As you have seen throughout this book, the past affects the present. You know this because once you (or your client) goes back to the life time with the original incident, the present time pattern or behavior simply vanishes.

But PLT allows us other possibilities as well! For instance, suppose you have come across a past life in which you had tremendous power and conviction but used it in a negative manner. Let's say that in this present lifetime, you would like to have those abilities of conviction and power but want to use them for the good and not the negative. In this case, you only need change the pictures in the past life.

For instance, if you had those abilities of power and conviction but used it to negative ends, you will see those pictures in the time film. Now change those pictures. Do not change the size or color of them at all. Just the content -- that is, what is inside the pictures. So, instead of you doing the negative actions as depicted in the time film, this time you change those time film pictures. Turn them to pictures of you having the same conviction and power, but using it to do good.

In fact, think of the ways in which you would use those resources (conviction and power) now, and add those resources to the past life pictures. So your past life time film pictures would now show you with those resources of power and conviction.

Now as your time film pictures have changed in accordance with your desires and tastes, you need to run those time film pictures with you inside of them so that you are actually feeling what is going on in those pictures. This is what is called being interiorized -- it is a sense of association, that you experience the feelings. Once you have done this then you can do the next step which is to make a copy of the past life pictures, and then move them up into present time. To do this, read and practice the material below in THE TIME LINE.

### THE TIME LINE

The time film (also referred to as the time line), is an ever swirling maelstorm of pictures and voices, and postulates and directives. If we consider that time itself is created by the mind as shown in the time line exercises, then we may also be creating the future. The future depends, at any one moment, on what we are thinking, what new directions, postulates and directives we decide to take in the present. This means that there is no absolute future.

The future is actually a promise of potential possibilities anyone of which can become realized and just as many to stay unrealized. The mind is a computer that acts on inputs. In this case, the inputs are past lives data. If you accept the past as it is in your mind, your mind will act on it and create parallel models in the present life. Then from the present life models come the future life models. These models create the patterns that will be experienced in the future. And if the present of futurepatterns are not what you want, then you have the option to alter it by altering the past lifetime from whence it comes.

The mind seems to track future lifetime possibilities just as a military computer would continuously compute the odds of a nuclear war or any new military action taking place on the planet.

Now in terms to past lives, there seems to be three major time periods:

1) The time when you first came into being and sought out a universe.

2) Involvement with various technological societies and space civilizations.

3) Involvement with bodies and your present entrapment on planet Earth.

It is possible that there are future life times that you have right now and that to some greater or lesser degree are influencing and being influenced by right now. This opens an interesting level of research. This research is being done now and will be published in a book as well as on Video and Audio cassettes.

## *THE TIME FILM AND HOW TO USE IT*

Another interesting technique of dealing with time is to find out how you organize time in your awareness. The way in which your organize time there is how you organize time on the outside - that is the external world.

Try this:

Get the image of brushing your hair about ten years ago. You do not have to actually get a memory of such a time, but only the concept. Now point to that concept - that memory picture of ten years ago. Notice where the picture appears.

Now get the image of brushing your hair about five years ago. Notice where the memory picture appears.

Now get the image of brushing your hair about two weeks ago.

Now get the image of brushing your hair right now in the present at this time.

Now get the idea of brushing your hair two weeks from now.

Now get the idea of brushing your hair five years from now. And finally get the idea of brushing your hair ten years on the future.

You will notice that there is some sort of pattern to how you organize time. This is what they must do in order to  organize and utilize time. We are the creators of time and we are the controllers with the proper tools and the techniques to do that.

For some people, their time lines are such that the memory is in back of them. Guess where anything after two weeks ago goes in terms of memory? Behind them. It is as if there is a time line that goes right through the person's back. Of course, this would also indicate that the future is right in front of them as well (which is usually the case).

These people are very time oriented because their physical body lies right in the middle of the time line. This is usually used by managers and accountant who need to keep a tight control on time and time expence.

Creative types tend to use a different time film orientation. The time film is out in front of them at a perpendicular to the face. The past might be on the left side of the head. The present right in front of the face and the future to the right of the face. Sometimes this film is reversed where past is on the right; the present in front of the face; and the future to the left. All on a straight line.

Talking about straight lines, this is the way in which the Western Civilization organizes time. In some parts of the orient it could be assumed that they have a time orientation that might be more circular.

The way time is organized within a culture or a species determines its communications as well. When two different species or cultures (different in the way that they organize and perceive time) interact, the difficulties and problems of this differing time perception and awareness becomes evident, even comical. Have you ever witnessed a conversation between an Arab and an American? The American thinks in terms of days, hours and weeks. When you say day to the American he thinks of tomorrow, 24 hours later. Day to the Arab might mean several days, perhaps even weeks.

I understand that during the Korean War, the United States sent negotiators to negotiate a peace settlement. The U.S rented a hotel for a week. The Koreans rented a villa for I believe it was five years. Americans usually have short time lines. This tends to compact time, so the perception is that a week goes by but it feels like a day. To the oriental mind, with the expanded time line, a week might seem like a month or months.

There are drawbacks to the way in which the time line is orientated. The American concept of time is to get something done as quick and as fast and as economical as possible. The problem is that people become fixated on the short term profits. No one has the long term vision. Everything becomes a bandage - a temporary cure.

The long term effects are ignored on the whole. For instance, the Amazon jungle is being torn up in record number for business and profit. Now exactly how much fresh oxygen does the Amazon jungle produce for the total benefit of everyone on earth? What will happen to the atmosphere, the planet, and life when that jungle is gone. Short term vision will destroy the entire planet in short speed.

This can be changed, however, by teaching others how to alter time. We don't really have to be in a rush. Life should be enjoyed. And you can attain this by simply understanding the way your time line works and then making the appropriate changes to the time line. Remember, the orientation of your time line and what you learn next will enable you to change time and your perception of it.

## _MOVING THE FUTURE TO THE PRESENT_

Look to where you put your future pictures. They may to the right of your face or in front of you. No matter where they are located, find a pleasant picture that is somewhere in your future. Another approach to this is to imagine something in the future that you would like to experience. Make sure that you think of this event as happening in the future. Find the mental picture or representation of that in your future line. Now quickly, take the picture/representation and move it from the future to the present time place on the time line (usually right in front of your face.)

Notice how you feel now that you have taken a future antici-pated event and brought it to present time?

You may notice that you feel as if you are actually in that event or situation now. This is because you took the way your brain anticipates the future and how it creates the present, and you are telling the brain to do that -- to take the future and make it happen now.

### *MOVING THE PRESENT TO THE PAST*

Look to where you put your present time pictures. They may appear right in front of your face. No matter where present time is located, find a habit, image, event or whatever that you have now in the present time and would like to get rid of. Find the pictures that are associated with that habit, image or event. They should be in the present time section of the time line. After all, you do have the habit or pattern in the present time, don't you? Now quickly, take the picture/representation and move it from the present time place on the time line (usually right in front of your face) to the past time place on the time line.

Notice how you feel now that you have taken a present problem and sent it into your past? You should feel like that habit or behavior is now in your past. You may feel like it was something you used to do but don't do now!

You will now notice that you feel as if whatever it was in your present time, you put into the past. The further you put the pictures into your past on the timefilm, the more distant and into the past you put your pictures. This present to the past phenomenon occurs because you took the way your brain organizes the past and how it creates the present. You then tell your brain to take what is in its present time organization and move it to its past time organization. The result being that what you experience in the present you now experience as having happened in the past.

### PAST TO THE PRESENT

Look to where you put your pictures of the past. They may be to the left or right of your face or in front of you. No matter where these pictures are located, find a pleasant picture that is somewhere in your past. Another approach to this is to imagine something in your past that you would like to experience now. Find the mental picture or representation of the experience in your past timeline. Now quickly, take the picture or representation and move it from the past to the present time place on the time line (usually right in front of your face.)

Notice how you feel now that you have taken a past event and brought it up to present time?

You may notice that you feel as if you are actually in that past event or situation now. This is because you are telling the brain to do that -- to take the past and make it happen now. Notice how full this past life to present life feeling is now.

### PRESENT TO THE FUTURE

Find where you put your present time pictures. They may right in front of your face. No matter where they are located, find a pleasant picture that is somewhere in your present. Make sure that you think of this event as happening now. Find the mental picture or representation of that in your present timeline. Now quickly, take the picture or representation and move it from the present to the future time/place on the time line (usually to the right of your face.)

Notice how you feel now that you have taken a present time experience and placed it into the future?

You may notice that you feel as if the present time experience is now somewhere in your future waiting to happen. This is because you told your brain to take the present and put it in the future.

## *PAST TO THE FUTURE*

Look to where you put your pictures of the past. They may be located to the left of your face. No matter where they are located, find a pleasant picture that is somewhere in your past. Another approach to this is to imagine something in your past that you would like to experience once again in your future. Now quickly, take the picture/representation and move it from the past to the future time place on the timeline (usually to the right of your face.)

Notice how you feel now that you have taken a past time event and brought it up to the future?

You may notice that you feel as if you are about to come on in the future, what you felt in your past. This is because you told your brain to take the past and put it in the future.

## *FUTURE TO THE PAST*

Look to where you put your future pictures. They may be to the right of your face. No matter where they are located, find a pleasant picture that is somewhere in your future. Another approach to this is to imagine something in the future that you would like to experience. Make sure that you think of this event as happening in the future.

Find the mental picture or representation of that in your future line.

Now quickly, take the picture/representation and move it from the future to the past time/place on the time line (usually to the left of your face.)

Notice how you feel now that you have taken a future anticipated event and brought it to past time?

You may notice that you feel as if you have already done what you saw in your future. By putting the future picture into your past timeline, you find that you feel like you are an "old pro" having done the future activity seemingly hundreds of times. This happens because you took the way your brain anticipates the future and how it organizes the past, and you are telling the brain to take the future and put it in your past.

# APPENDIX 1

# THE TERMINOLOGY
# OF
# PAST LIFE THERAPY

The following is a list of terms that are used throughout this book. As in any field of knowledge, it has become important that a terminology be developed. Here it is :

## TABLE 1 - PLT TERMINOLOGY

Agreement -   The acceptance of a situation or oc curence. Agreement is the basis of reality.

Attention -   The dynamic focusing of awareness onto a particular item or event.

Aura -   The energy field that surrounds all living things.

Awareness -   The level of understanding and perception that a person possesses.

Being(ness) -       All the levels of awareness, perception and
                    knowledge.

Comm Lines -        The communication/energy lines of force
                    that contain information and connect all
                    living things to each other.

Conscious Mind-     The one-tenth awareness of our mind. It is
                    limited in its abilities and actually acts as
                    an analytical filter deciding and recogniz
                    ing patterns of energy, for instance, that a
                    chair is a chair and is not to be confused
                    with a tree.

Consciousness-      The mental and spiritual factors of the
                    being.

Content -           The internal information related to the
                    environment or perception. For example,
                    in a picture, content would be the shapes,
                    colors, tones, i.e., the trees, the people, the
                    landscape and whatever else is in the
                    picture.

Context -           This is the external information related to
                    the picture.  Whereas content is the actual
                    information, context is the way in which
                    that data is stored, used, and handled. An
                    example of content is the information that
                    a person says. An example of context,
                    is not what the person says (content), but
                    the way in which he says it (context).

Decision -      a decision is the same as a postulate. A postulate is a command, a directive. By making certain decisions, one changes ones life. A drastic postulate may change a life drastically.

Duration -      The amount of time it takes to complete something such as a cycle of action, chore or event.

Enactment -      This is where a person enacts a scene from some past life in the present life. One fellow used to enact dying whenever he couldn't get his way. Sure enough, in a past life he was a criminal. He got convicted of murder, couldn't have his way, and was condemned to death by hanging. The very type of death that he enacted.

Energy Charge-      This is the energy that was originally cre ated during the primary or original inci dent. The energy or force done to the per son is an actual energy charge contained in the memory of the original or primary incident. (See Force).

Event -      The actual incident in present life or past life that causes difficulties and problems in the present life.

Exteriorization-      The ability to be in an 'astral projected' dissociated, objective state of beingness and mind.

Filters -        These are the mental and emotional and
                 physical factors that tone down and limit
                 energy, perception or responses.

Force -          The use of energy, communication or
                 power to make something occur. Over
                 whelming force is more power than is re
                 quired to make a desired effect occur.

Hostile Act -    An act or event done by a person against
                 himself or others that limits, hinders or
                 destroys his own or another's goals or in-
                 tentions.

Implant -        A specific behavior change technique
                 usually using electronics and energy
                 forces. Found in the early time usually
                 Middle and Earliest Atlantis as well as
                 on other planets.

Incident -       Same as event.

Interiorization -   opposite of exteriorization. Inside and
                 associated to feelings and situations. This
                 is where one tends to be emotional feeling
                 and anything but rational.

Models -         These are the behavioral examples that
                 surround us. They can be people, parents,
                 teachers and mentors. Anything from
                 which one derives a new behavior,
                 insight or perception (whether good or
                 bad) is a model. Earth seems to have
                 mainly bad models.

Memory Bank -    The reservoir of pictures and memories.

Original -    This is the very first incident or event in
Incident    which a pattern, behavior or habit became
    developed. This is the incident you want
    to erase and clear in order to release the
    habit, behavior, or pattern.

Past Life -    The ability to bring up to conscious aware
Recall    ness past life memories and images.

Past Life -    The process or technique of returning a
Therapy    person's awareness back to the moment of
    impact (the primary or original incident)
    which most likely occured in an earlier
    life, in order to discharge and erase the
    incident. By doing so, immediate changes
    in behavior and perception occur.

Pattern -    A habit, or behavior that is repeated pre
    cisely each time in the environment that
    habit was created in. For example, a person
    who sees others smoking and then goes
    through an internal pattern himself (per
    haps seeing himself lighting a cigarette,
    then hearing a voice say "Go for it!" and
    then feeling the urge to smoke, resulting in
    his lighting a cigarette.

Postulate -    A decision, a directive. For example, in a
    past life incident the person may have
    trusted in others and they betrayed him.
    The betrayal leads to his death. At the time

of death, he postulates "I can't trust anybody!" Now in the present life time, he is antisocial, untrusting of others, incapable of close contact or relationships. The root of this pattern of his life being the postulate "I can't trust anybody!" This postulate acts as a hypnotic command to a hypnotized subject.

Primary -

same as original incident that created a particular behavior.

Release -

The clearing and erasure of the energy charge that got formed when the first incident - the original or primary incident - occurred. The energy charge got stored along with the incident throughout lifetimes and bodies.

Secondary -

This is any lifetime that comes after the primary or original incident. For instance, a boy has an original incident of a man shaking his hand in front of the boy's face. Then the boy gets hit by the man. The pain causes the energy charge to get stored. Now all that is necessary is for a man to shake his fist in front of the boy's face in this life time to get the boy to react-emotionally. The secondary events have emotion and feeling and reactions but not the original pain or force that was in the primary incident.

| | |
|---|---|
| Subconscious - Mind | That part of the awareness of the individual that keeps the body intact (i.e., keeps the heart beating and the body breathing, without need of the conscious mind. |
| Time Film - | Also known as the Time Line, Time Track and other names. It is the total record of the existence of the being in this universe. |
| Trigger - | Any picture, sound, experience etc, that causes a past life pattern or habit turn-on and come into manifestation. |
| Unconscious - Mind | Same as the Subconscious mind. |
| Unconsciousness - | The filtering out of the conscious mind and awareness. This could be due to physical force (such as a blow to the head), hypnosis, drugs, poisons, and implants. |

ADVANCED MIND TECHNOLOGIES
PRODUCT AND PRICE LIST
P.O. BOX 1403
NASHUA, NEW HAMPSHIRE 03061
1-603-883-4903 (Orders Only)

CASSETTE TAPES BY RICHARD A. GREENE

## *ASTRAL PROJECTION*
**$9.95 1. The Real You - Beyond the Body**
This lecture reveals the immortal 'YOU'. When the body dies, you will still exist...but who are you then? This tape answers this and other questions.

**$9.95 2. How To Astral Project Through Distance and Space**
This lecture reveals the techniques to project your consicousness over distance no matter whether it be next door or millions of miles through space.

**$9.95 3. How To Astral Project Through Time**
Time travel through astral projection. This tape teaches you how!

**$9.95 4. How To Astral Project Into Past Lives**
Use astral projection techniques to remember your past lives! A remarkable tape!

## *PSYCHIC HEALING AND PSYCHIC ENERGY*
**$9.95 5. The Life Force Energy -- How To Develop And Direct It**
The Life Force Energy surrounds and animates all living things. This tape teaches you how to use the LFE in your everyday life to increase your physical vitality, reduce stress and much, much more.

**$9.95 6. Psychic Healing - Healing Through Color, Auras and The LFE**
This tape teaches you how to use the Life Force Energy along with colors and the aura, in order to positively influence your own health and the health of others.

## *HIDDEN KNOWLEDGE*
**$9.95 7. The True Purpose of Planet Earth**
Some people think earth is a classroom, but this tape may just change your mind. In this tape, you learn techniques to go back in time to when you, as an immortal soul, first came to planet Earth, and for what purpose.

## $9.95 8. The Mysteries Of This Universe

In order to be a spiritually evolved person, and use your spiritual abilities, you must know something about the universe you are presently existing in. In this tape, you will learn the factors that create this universe as well as other ones.

## $9.95 9. How To Obtain Personal Power

Many people feel that they do not have the power to control or change their lives. This tape teaches you the laws of personal power so you can have power in your life now. Empower yourself!

## $9.95 10. What Really Happens Between Lifetimes

It is interesting how many books have been written about past lives but nobody seems to know the truth about what happens in the "between lifetimes period." This is very vital and important information for your spiritual development.

## $9.95 11. The True Story Behind Karma and Reincarnation

By understanding how karma and reincarnation actually work, you will have a greater awareness of your present strengths, weaknesses, and goals.

## _PSYCHIC AND SPIRITUAL DEVELOPMENT_
## $9.95 12. How To Develop and Use Telepathy

Telepathy is the communication process of sending thoughts, images, and energy from one person's mind to another mind. This tape teaches you the techniques to develop telepathy. So who needs telephones?

## $9.95 13. How To Develop and Use Psychokinesis

Psychokinesis is the ability to use your mind to influence and affect matter such as bending metal keys, or moving objects using only thought. This tape teaches you the techniques to develop the power of psychokinesis.

## $9.95 14. How To See Auras

Auras are the energy fields that surround all living things. By learning to see auras, you can tell the emotional, mental and physical status of any individual. All the techniques you need to see auras are included in this tape.

## $9.95 15. How To Communicate With Your Higher Self

The Higher Self is your true inner spiritual being. When you are in touch with your Higher Self, you are in touch with the highest levels of spiritual knowledge and being. This tape teaches you how to communicate with your spiritual Higher Self.

## PSYCHIC POWERS

**$9.95 16. How To Develop Invisibility**
Invisibility is the ability to alter your features by using the Life Force Energy to change the way that light emits from your aura. This tape teaches you how it is done!

**$9.95 17. How to Develop and Use Your Psychic Powers**
This tape explains what psychic powers are, how and why they work, and how to develop them. Some of the abilities covered are telepathy and psychic healing.

**$9.95 18. How To Attract Wealth and Prosperity**
Few people understand the laws of wealth and prosperity. This is one of the reasons why most people lack the wealth they desire. This tape contains exercises to prepare your consciousness to attract the very wealth and the $$$ you need!

**$9.95 19. How To Handle The Problems In Your Life**
Wouldn't it be nice to finally handle the problems in your life so that you can stop worrying and move on to more productive and fun things? This tape teaches you what a problem really is, and the methods to solve each and every problem that is in your life. This tape is a must!

**$9.95 20. Death - The Final Mystery**
What is death? Why does it happen? What occurs after death? This tape contains exercises and data researched through past life therapy by Richard Greene. Included in this tape are exercises to help you overcome the grief, fear and worry associated with death.

**$9.95 21. How To Control Time**
What is time? Where does it come from? These questions and more are asked and answered in this tape. As you learn and understand the source of where time comes from, you are also taught how to control time to get things done.

**$9.95 22. How To Gain Control Of Your Life**
At some point in our lives, we all go through a time where we feel that we have lost the purpose which is the very reason why we are on this planet. This is when we feel out of control. This tape explains how and why we lose control of our life and the techniques necessary to regain control. This is an important tape!

**$9.95 23. How To Manifest The Things You Want In Your Life**
It seems that very few people ever get what they want out of life. People who do

C - 3

are using laws of consciousness whether they realize it or not. This tape teaches you all the laws necessary to bring your wishes and dreams into reality. A "must have" tape!!!

## BOOKS AND MANUALS BY RICHARD A. GREENE
**Please include $2.00 (U.S.) for postage and handling.**

### $14.95 The Handbook of Astral Power
Formerly titled *The Handbook of Astral Projection*, this book is the classic on astral projection developed by Richard A. Greene. It actually teaches you how to astral project using easy to learn techniques that have been developed over two decades.

Hypnotic tactics and strategies of Exteriorization and Astral Projection for fast behavior and pattern changes are covered. Also covered are important uses of AP for pain control, stress reduction and much more. In addition, you can see your progress in AP by taking the 'TOUR GUIDE TO THE SUN AND MOON' test at the end of the book.

**2. The Magic of Psychic Healing $14.95**
**3. The Magic of Past Life Therapy $14.95**

### AUDIO CASSETTE TAPE SEMINARS by Richard A. Greene

### 1. Hypnotic Past Life Therapy $95.00
Consists of eight tapes teaching you how the techniques and applications of Past Life Therapy works and how to start your own Past Life Therapy business.

### 2. Psychic Healing $95.00
Consists of eight tapes teaching you how the techniques and applications of Psychic Healing (also known as Therapeutic Touch) works. Included will be how to start your own Psychic Healing business.

### The Astral Projection Course - Level 1 $39.95
This course includes audio tapes #2, #3, #4, and the Handbook of Astral Power. Save over $5.00

### The Communication Course - Level 1   $69.95  (Consists of 6 tapes)
Includes information and techniques on the cycles of communication, how to influence others via communication, communicate with others telepathically, and so much more.

C - 4

ADVANCED MIND TECHNOLOGIES
PRODUCT ORDER FORM
P.O. BOX 1403
NASHUA, NEW HAMPSHIRE 03061
1-603-883-4903 (VISA and MasterCard Orders only)
Or, please mail this order form with the products you desire checked off. Also, make all money payable in U.S. dollars please.

Please include $4.00 for Postage and Handling!

## ASTRAL PROJECTION
___ $9.95 1. The Real You - Beyond The Body
___ $9.95 2. How To Astral Project Through Distance and Space
___ $9.95 3. How To Astral Project Through Time
___ $9.95 4. How To Astral Project Into Past Lives
___ $9.95 5. The Life Force Energy -- How to Develop And Direct It
___ $9.95 6. Psychic Healing - Healing Through Colors, Auras, and the LFE

## HIDDEN KNOWLEDGE
___ $9.95 7. The True Purpose of Planet Earth
___ $9.95 8. The Mysteries Of This Universe
___ $9.95 9. How To Obtain Personal Power
___ $9.95 10. What Really Happens Between Lifetimes
___ $9.95 11. The True Story Behind Karma and Reincarnation

## PSYCHIC AND SPIRITUAL DEVELOPMENT
___ $9.95 12. How To Develop and Use Telepathy
___ $9.95 13. How To Develop and Use Psychokinesis
___ $9.95 14. How To See Auras
___ $9.95 15. How To Communicate With Your Higher Self

## PSYCHIC POWERS
___ $9.95 16. How To Develop Invisibility
___ $9.95 17. How To Develop And Use Your Psychic Powers
___ $9.95 18. How To Attract Wealth and Prosperity
___ $9.95 19. How To Handle The Problems In Your Life
___ $9.95 20. Death - The Final Mystery
___ $9.95 21. How To Control Time
___ $9.95 22. How To Gain Control Of Your Life
___ $9.95 23. How To Manifest The Things You Want In Your LIfe

## Video Cassette Tape Courses (VHS Format Only)

### RICHARD A. GREENE HYPNOSIS PRODUCTS
National Organization of Trained and Certified Hypnotists

**VIDEOS (All videos are $75.00 each. Please include $6.00 Postage and Handling)**

### 1. Advanced Hypnotic Inductions
This video covers various rapid induction techniques, as well as hypnotic language patterns for fast and powerful hypnotic inductions.

### 2. Hypnotic Language Patterns
This video covers how the mind and body relates to language and how to use language for hypnotic inductions and therapy.

### 3. Elements of Hypnotic Therapy
This video covers the step by step procedures of how to deal with the unconsciousand conscious minds for effective long-lasting therapy.

### 4. Bio-Energy Hypnosis Inductions
This video covers the application of the Life Force Energy for rapid inductions. Even the toughest people to hypnotize, are easily hypnotized with the bio-energy.

### 5. Bio-Energy Hypnosis Therapy
This video covers the fastest therapy available - Bio-Energy Hypnosis. Imagine stopping smoking, overeating, fear, depression, etc. in less than 10 minutes.

### 6. Fast Hypnotic Inductions
This video covers fast and exotic inductions. You'll never have to spend a lot of time hypnotizing a client again.

### 7. Hypnotic Patterns of Time Distortion
This video covers how to use time distortion, past, present and future time, for quick therapy and healing. Hypnosis is easy when you can alter time!

### 8. Hypnosis and Metaphor
This video covers how to use stories and metaphors for long term healing. Hypnotic Metaphors are fast and effective with everybody, but especially resistive clients and children.

C - 6

### 9. Hypnosis and Pattern Interrupts

This video covers how to discover mental patterns of others and use them by leverage and interruption, to effect hypnosis, and fast and effective change. This is especially effective using conversation.

### 10. Hypnosis and Rapid Phobia Cure

This video covers how phobias occur in the mind, and how to alter them in less than 20 minutes - no matter how severe the phobia. Actual demonstrations illustrate the techniques.

### 11. Hypnosis and Rapid Procrastination Cure

This video covers why and how procrastination happens, and fast effective techniques to change the procrastinator to a doer. Actual demonstrations illustrate the techniques.

### 12. Hypnosis and Advanced Modeling Techniques

If you want to be the best, find the best and copy them. This video covers how to model the best behaviors and habits of others and make them yours, or transfer them to a client in less than an hour.

### 13. Hypnosis and Stop Smoking Techniques

This video covers several approaches for stopping smoking. All techniques are explained and demonstrated.

### 14. Hypnosis and Weight Reduction Techniques

This video covers several approaches for stopping overeating. All techniques are explained and demonstrated.

### 15. Hypnotic Techniques for Creativity and the Awakening of Genius

This video covers several approaches for development of genius and creativity. Learn to never be stopped by a problem or difficulty again.

### 16. Hypnosis and Unconscious Parts Negotiation Techniques

This video covers several approaches of negotiating with the unconscious mind in order for it to change and alter unwanted behaviors in yourself or others. All techniques are explained and demonstrated.

### COMING SOON ON VIDEO (VHS FORMAT ONLY)
### 17. Hypnotic Sales Techniques
### 18. Kinesthetic Hypnosis

19. Hypnosis and Advanced Past Life Therapy Techniques
20. Hypnosis and Advanced Techniques of Exteriorization/Astral Projection
21. Hypnosis and Psychic Powers Development
22. Hypnosis and Age Regression
23. Hypnotic Time Distortion Techniques
24. Hypnotic Pre-Natal Techniques
25. Hypnosis and Relationship Changes
26. Hypnosis and Skill and Ability Enhancement
27. Hypnosis Stage Show Techniques
28. How to Make Over $100,000 In Your Own Hypnosis Business
29. How To Market Your Hypnosis Talents and Business
30. Hypnosis and Self-Esteem/Self-Confidence
31. Hypnosis and Spiritual Development
32. Hypnosis and Tactics of Triggering Behaviors
33. Hypnosis and Post-Hypnotic Suggestions
34. Hypnosis and Power Rapport
35. Hypnosis and Trance States
36. Hypnotic Techniques to Cure Insomnia
37. Non-Induction Hypnosis
38. Hypnosis and Future Lives
39. Hypnotic Techniques for Instant Pain Control
40. Hypnotic Filters of the Mind
41. Hypnotic States of Being
42. Hypnotic Power Leverage
43. Conscious Mind Hypnosis
44. Hypnotic Fast Behavior Change
45. Subliminal Hypnotic Language Patterns
46. Hypnotic Language Techniques to Change Beliefs
47. Hypnosis and Reality - Tactics of Reality
48. Hypnosis and The Attitude of Wealth and Riches
49. Hypnosis and Addiction Control
50. Hypnotic Techniques for Behavior and Emotion Transformation
51. Hypnotic Techniques for the Transformation of Meaning
52. Hypnosis and Possession-Unconscious Mind Parts Therapy
53. Hypnosis and Performing Arts

*Many new video and audio cassette courses are being developed. Call 1-603-883-4903 for titles and prices.*

**Name:** _____
                    **(Please Print)**

**Address:**_____

**City & State:**_____

**Zip:**_____

**Tel. #: (   )_____**

**Visa/MC #:**

**Exp. Date:**